LET'S Laugh TOGETHER

ACTIVITIES FOR LISTENING COMPREHENSION

Alexis Gerard Finger
Gregory A. Barnes

DREXEL UNIVERSITY, PHILADELPHIA

COLLIER
MACMILLAN

Library of Congress Cataloging-in-Publication Data

Gerard Finger, Alexis.
 Let's laugh together.

 1. English language—Textbooks for foreign
speakers. 2. Humor in education. 3. Listening.
I. Barnes, Gregory Allen. II. Title.
PE1128.G385 1988   428.3'4   87-30837
ISBN 0-02-337670-8

Collier Macmillan Canada, Inc.

Design: *Ros Herion Freese*
Illustrations: *Anna Veltfort*

Some of the jokes appearing in this book are reprinted
with the permission of Art Buchwald, *Los Angeles Times*,
and Joey Adams, who gives his permission "with love
and laughs."

Printing: 1 2 3 4 5 6 7   Year: 8 9 0 1 2 3 4

Collier Macmillan
866 Third Avenue
New York, NY 10022

Printed in the U.S.A.

ISBN 0-02-337670-8

Acknowledgments

For giving us lots of laughs, we thank Irv, Andrew, and Scott Finger, and Sandy, Roby, and Stephen Barnes. For ongoing scouting, we thank Laurence Gerard, Henrietta Gerard, Ede Cheeseman, and Stanley Goldfarb.

For guidance, we thank Joey Adams, Isaac Asimov, Fran Leibowitz, and Art Buchwald. And for invaluable contributions and tremendous generosity, we sincerely thank Joey Adams and Art Buchwald.

Contents

Dear Instructor:

We offer you a toast. You've worked long and hard to help English-as-a-Second-Language students master a complex language and to provide them with insights into a many-faceted culture. We like to think we are offering your class the final challenge: mastering American humor. If you can teach your advanced students, who think they're already pretty good at English, the what and the why of our humor, they will be forever in your debt.

Let's Laugh Together, our tape and text program, is designed to dispel some of the mysteries that obscure this fascinating reflection of our culture. Our presentation of American jokes is on tape, so that your students are exposed to humor as they are most likely to encounter it—spoken (not read) by comedians, teachers, and American friends. We can't promise that you will love every joke you hear or roar with laughter at the punch lines. Even the best comedians bomb sometimes. What we do promise is a rich variety of vocabulary, topics, and activities providing innumerable springboards for cultural discussions and listening-comprehension exercises to keep even your top students on their toes.

So save your coffee for another course. You won't need it here to stay alert. Your students and the material in hand will keep you all thinking, talking, and a good deal of the time, laughing together.

Dear Student:

Congratulations! You've made it. You should be pleased with yourself for having come far enough in the adventure of learning English to start tearing down the last barrier separating you and your English-speaking friends: American humor. All you need now is the ability to moan, groan, frown, smile, and laugh—because that is what you will be expected to do.

Let's Laugh Together is an exciting challenge facing you. It is filled with lots of activities designed for thinking, listening, laughing, and fun. Don't worry when you don't understand or appreciate a joke. Just remember that you are not alone. Even Americans don't always get the jokes they hear. Not everybody likes the same thing, thinks the same way, or perceives the world similarly, and these differences affect people's responses to jokes. Many Americans find themselves frowning at jokes or saying, "Sorry, but I don't get it," or "Excuse me, could you say that again?" or simply, "What's so funny?" And you can certainly do the same.

So just relax, learn what to listen for, learn how to react, and go ahead and laugh if the joke amuses you. By the time you finish this book, you'll probably feel like writing your own jokes.

Using the Book

Let's Laugh Together: Activities for Listening Comprehension can be used as a main text in listening-comprehension courses or as a supplementary text in general English classes. Its primary objectives are to

1. provide students with opportunities to hear "authentic" American humor in the form they are likely to hear it—spoken;
2. further develop listening skills that students can apply to other situations;
3. expand students' vocabularies;
4. increase students' knowledge and understanding of America and its people through its humor.

Organization of the Text

The material in *Let's Laugh Together* increases in difficulty as students advance through the units. The introductory unit is presented as a reading selection in order to acquaint students with the language and activities they will encounter in the other units. To facilitate comprehension and mastery, each of the first six units is divided into two parts in order to limit the amount of vocabulary and jokes covered. The last four units are longer in order to challenge more advanced students as they become more able to sustain their concentration over longer periods of time.

Each unit contains five sections: *Get Ready; Now, Let's Laugh; Check Yourself; Follow It Up;* and *Take It Further.*

Get Ready (Pre-Listening Activities)

LET'S TALK.
What? An introduction to the topics of the unit and questions to stimulate interest.
How? Read this aloud, or have students read it to themselves. Then discuss.

BUILD YOUR VOCABULARY.
What? A list of key words in context. Additional boxed list of words to be checked in the Glossary.
How? Have students read the sentences with the key words, and have them try to predict the meaning from context. Have students look at the boxed words, guess their meanings, and then consult the Glossary.

PREVIEW THESE SENTENCES.
What? Examples of sentences taken directly from the script.
Why? To familiarize students with some of the speech and vocabulary they will hear on the tape.
How? Read the key sentences, or have students listen to the cassette. Then have students fill in the missing words in their text.

Now, Let's Laugh *(Listening-Comprehension Activities)*
What? The cassette recording of the script followed by short-answer questions.
How? Have students read the questions, take notes while listening to the cassette, and then answer the true/false questions.

Check Yourself *(Listening-Comprehension Exercises)*
COMPREHENSION CHECK.
What? The cassette recording again.
How? Have students read the questions, listen to the cassette, and then answer the questions orally or in writing or both.

WHAT'S MISSING?
What? The cassette recording again.
How? Listen to the cassette, and then complete the jokes with the missing words.

Follow It Up *(Post-Listening Activities)*
WORKING TOGETHER.
What? Pair work requiring the use of new vocabulary.
How? Have partners write sentences, questions, or summaries. (See specific instructions in each unit.)

FINDING SYNONYMS.
What? Vocabulary and comprehension activity.
How? Have students find words from the unit that are similar in meaning to those underlined. (These exercises can be done at home.)

COMPLETING SENTENCES.
What? Vocabulary and comprehension activity.
How? Have students fill in the sentences with vocabulary introduced in the unit. (These exercises can be done at home.)

Take It Further
What? Activities, discussion questions, and additional jokes.
How? Answer questions, analyze and recreate jokes, tell personal jokes. (See specific instructions in each unit.)

The text contains a written introduction, ten listening-comprehension units, tapescripts of the monologues, an answer key, and a glossary. The cassettes that accompany the textbook contain the key sentences, the monologues, and the true/false questions for each unit.

A.G.F.
G.A.B.

The Structure and Categories of Jokes

PART I

"Frankly, it surprises me, too. He hated the book."

Get Ready

Do the GET READY activities in each unit before reading the comedian's jokes and commentary. These activities will help you understand the comedian.

1. LET'S TALK. Whatever country you live in, you are going to hear people telling jokes. Although they may be difficult for you to understand, jokes are often very revealing and informative. You can learn much about the United States and its people when you learn to understand American jokes. Let's be specific: What kinds of things can you learn?

2. BUILD YOUR VOCABULARY. Try to guess the meanings of the words in bold italics.

1. It's **illogical** to go outside in your bathing suit when there's snow on the ground.
2. Fred **exaggerated** when he said he made $200. He only made $150 on the job.
3. The way you see or tell things is your **point of view**.
4. You know so much about cars. Who taught you the **ins and outs** of fixing cars?
5. I'm sorry you failed your driving test, but don't **despair**. If you continue to practice your driving, I'm sure you'll pass next time.
6. One of the main **ingredients** in pizza is cheese.
7. There has been an **alteration** in my thinking. For many reasons, I have changed my mind.

Here are some additional words you will need to know. Check the Glossary for any of these words you don't understand.

astonished	snarled	unveil
remark	twist	villain
resemble	unexpected	yelp

---

3. PREVIEW THESE SENTENCES. Read the Preview Sentences below. Make sure you understand the meaning of the underlined words before you continue reading.

1. Clearly, the dog was understanding the picture, for he <u>snarled</u> softly when the <u>villain</u> spoke, yelped joyously at the funny <u>remarks</u>, and so on.
2. When we take appropriate or expected behavior and <u>twist</u> it, alter it, <u>exaggerate</u> it, and stretch it, we produce laughter.
3. As we suggested before, the main <u>ingredient</u> in every good joke is a sudden <u>alteration</u> in <u>point of view</u>.

Now, Let's Laugh

Read the following monologue, and decide if the statements at the end are true or false. You may check your answers on page 157.

You are about to read an old American joke.

> Once when Jack Jones was in a movie theater, he noticed that the man in front of him had his arm around the neck of a large dog in the seat next to him. Clearly, the dog was understanding the picture, for he snarled softly when the villain spoke, yelped joyously at the funny remarks, and so on.
>
> Jack leaned forward and tapped the man on the shoulder.
>
> "Pardon me, sir," he said, "but I am astonished at your dog's behavior."
>
> The man turned around and said, "Frankly, it surprises me, too. He hated the book."

Are you laughing? Well, if you aren't, it's probably because you aren't familiar with the way Americans treat their pets, especially their dogs and cats. Many Americans regard them as friends and even talk to them. Of course, most of us don't believe our dogs can read. But the owner of the dog in this joke does, and that's what makes it funny. The unexpected or illogical statement or behavior makes us laugh.

When we take appropriate or expected behavior and twist it, alter it, exaggerate it, and stretch it, we produce laughter. If nothing in a joke resembles something that's real or familiar to us, we find nothing funny to laugh at. It's a joke that comes close to some truth, or to what many people believe is true, that makes us laugh.

Of course, in order to recognize the twist, the altered or the exaggerated point of view, you have to be familiar with what is normal and usual behavior. For example, in order to appreciate the joke about the dog, it helps to know two things about Americans: (1) they treat their dogs like friends; and (2) they often compare movies they've seen with the books on which these movies were based. But how can you know these things if you haven't lived in a culture for a long time? Where does that leave you? Well, right now it leaves you with us as your guide, ready to tell you the ins and outs of American humor: the structure of a joke, the categories of jokes, and the importance of the presentation, or delivery, of a joke. Then, while we're telling you various jokes, we'll unveil many details you need to know about American behavior and American culture.

So don't despair. By the time you finish this text, you will know more about American humor than the average American. You may even feel like writing your own material. And we'll all be laughing together!

The first thing you should understand is the structure of a joke, which is really quite simple. As we suggested before, the main ingredient in every good joke is a sudden alteration in point of view.

Sometimes the joke is short and the change comes quickly, and sometimes it's long and builds to a high point—a climax, like a short story. But instead of the expected ending, the final statement, called the punch line, is unexpected or illogical. And the surprise usually causes us to laugh just as we did (or should have) when the owner of the dog said, "He hated the book."

Read the next joke and see if you can spot the alteration in point of view.

> "Poor Mr. Jones!" cried Mrs. Smith. "Did you hear what happened to him? He tripped at the top of the steps, fell down the stairs, banged his head, and died."
> "Died?" said Mrs. Robinson, in a shocked voice.
> "Died," repeated Mrs. Smith, "and he broke his new glasses, too!"

Did you expect that ending? I hope not! The important information here is that a man died. Who cares about his broken glasses! Surely it is inappropriate in any culture to care about a material object like glasses when a human being has died. So what makes you laugh is that the build-up didn't prepare you for the punch line that was illogical and inappropriate.

Such jokes that end with unexpected punch lines are called anti-climax jokes. The joke about the dog and the joke about Mr. Jones fall in this category.

Before you read further, let's stop and see if you understand what's going on. Read the following statements, and decide if they are true or false.

Write your answers here.

1. According to the joke, the dog in the movie theater hated the movie.

   _____

2. A good joke has a logical and expected ending. _____

3. The punch line in the joke about Mr. Jones is: "Died," repeated Mrs.

   Smith, "and he broke his new glasses, too!" _____

Check Yourself

Re-read the monologue before you do the exercises. When you have finished, check your answers on pages 157 and 3.

1. COMPREHENSION CHECK. Answer each question with a sentence.

1. What two things do you need to know about Americans in order to appreciate the joke about the dog? _____

_____

2. How does understanding normal behavior in America help you understand American jokes? _____

_____

3. What is the main ingredient in every good joke? _____

_____

2. WHAT'S MISSING? Complete the jokes using words from the monologue. You may need to re-read the jokes.

Once _____ Jack _____ was in _____ movie

_____, he _____ that the _____ in _____

of him had his _____ around the _____ of a large

_____ in the _____ next to him. _____, the dog

was _____ the _____, for he _____ softly when the

_____ spoke, yelped _____ at the _____ remarks,

and _____ _____.

Jack _____ _____ and tapped the man on the

_____.

"_____ me, sir," he _____, "but I _____

_____ at your _____ behavior."

The man _____ around and said, "_____, it

_____ me, too. He _____ the _____.

Follow It Up

Apply your new knowledge and use your new vocabulary by doing the exercises that follow.

1. WORKING TOGETHER. In pairs, write sentences with at least eight words from this part of the Introduction.

_____

_____

_____

_____

_____

_____

_____

_____

_____

_____

2. FINDING SYNONYMS. Write a word or expression from this unit that is similar in meaning to the words underlined.

1. Please tell us your <u>opinion</u>. _____

2. I didn't expect such a <u>change</u> in Bob's appearance. _____

3. I was so <u>surprised</u> when I heard Ben won the contest. _____

4. Do you think Ruth <u>looks like</u> me? _____

5. Her visit was <u>a surprise</u>. _____

3. COMPLETING SENTENCES. Fill in the blanks with words from this list. Be sure to use the correct form.

| ingredient | villain | snarl |
| twist | remark | ins and outs |

1. This is a new _____. You usually never agree with me.

2. Can you teach me the _____ of banking in three weeks?

3. Does the _____ always wear a black hat in the movies?

4. I didn't like his _____ about my new job. At least I have a job!

5. What's the main _____ in this chicken dish?

6. Wendy got scared when that big dog _____ at her.

"If you'd really like to get me something for my birthday, I'd like a plane."

Get Ready

Do the GET READY activities in each unit before reading the comedian's jokes and commentary. These activities will help you understand the comedian.

1. BUILD YOUR VOCABULARY. Try to guess the meanings of the words in bold italics.

1. I won't accept your **insult**. You have no right to say I am stupid.
2. Michael Jackson is quite an **entertainer**. He can sing, dance, and act.
3. A family was celebrating Christmas in the first **scene** in the movie.
4. We **judged** you unfairly. We thought you were selfish, but we were wrong.
5. He **oversimplified** the situation. Actually, it's much more complex.
6. Do you know the actual number of people who drink soda every day? Do you have any **statistics**?

7. Jane can't **recall** what she did last Sunday. Do you remember?
8. I hope I haven't **offended** you. I didn't mean to hurt your feelings when I said you looked ill.

Here are some additional words you will need to know. Check the Glossary for any of these words you don't understand.

agency	comedian	malicious
bunch	exaggerate	poke fun at
Cadillac	herd	stereotype

---

2. PREVIEW THESE SENTENCES. Read the Preview Sentences below. Make sure you understand the meaning of the underlined words before you continue reading.

1. In America, as in many other countries, people are often judged by how much money they have, but just as important, they are judged by the number of friends they have.
2. Regional and ethnic jokes are based on stereotypes, which are exaggerated and oversimplified beliefs or opinions about a group of people.
3. Two Texans returning from lunch stopped before the window of a Cadillac automobile agency.

Now, Let's Laugh

Read the following monologue, and decide if the statements at the end are true or false. You may check your answers on page 157.

Another category of jokes is the "put-down." It is similar to the anticlimax joke because the punch line is also unexpected. In this case, however, where sympathy is the expected response, sudden, further insult is added instead. For example, there's the story about a famous entertainer named Al Jolson, who was known to be a hard man to work with.

When a young movie director told the actor that he could do a scene better, Mr. Jolson stopped what he was doing, stared at the young director angrily, and said, "Listen, kid, I've got a million dollars. What do you have?"

The director looked at him and said quietly, "Friends."

Now that's what we call a put-down. In America, as in many other countries, people are often judged by how much money they have, but just as important, they are judged by the number of friends they have. A man or a woman with no friends is judged to be a poor person indeed! So in this joke, Mr. Jolson was made to look very small and very poor.

The next group of jokes falls into the category of wordplays or puns. Some words in English have double meanings. By using different meanings of the same word or a similar meaning or a similar sound of different words, we create jokes. This explanation probably sounds complicated, but an example should simplify it.

This pun is built around two words that sound exactly alike but have different meanings. The two characters in the joke are Joe and Sue.

JOE: Look at that bunch of cows.
SUE: Not *bunch*. *Herd*.
JOE: Heard of what?
SUE: Herd of cows.
JOE: Sure I've heard of cows.
SUE: No, I mean a cow herd.
JOE: What do I care if a cow heard? I haven't said anything to be ashamed of!

What's funny here? Well, Joe doesn't know that a group of cows is called a *herd*—h-e-r-d—and not a *bunch*. When Sue corrects him, Joe thinks she's saying *heard*—h-e-a-r-d—the past tense of *hear*. Of course he has "heard" of cows, and he doesn't care if a cow "heard" (that is, listened to) what he was saying.

If you're still having trouble with wordplays and puns in English, don't worry. You'll have other opportunities to hear and analyze these jokes in the units that follow. Now let's move along to a group of jokes that are easier to understand.

Regional and ethnic jokes are based on stereotypes, which are exaggerated and oversimplified beliefs or opinions about a group of people. Often there is a small bit of truth in these stereotypes, because some people of a particular group may possess similar characteristics, although many others won't. Fortunately or unfortunately, the statistics don't matter. Jokesters and comedians feel that stereotypes make excellent "butts of humor"—that is, objects, people or groups of people that are being made fun of for the purpose of embarrassing them and causing laughter.

Ethnic jokes are about people of different races, religions, or nationalities, and they can be insulting and harmful. You may not want to hear one told about your own ethnic group.

Regional jokes are usually less malicious. Here's one that pokes fun at Texans (you know, people who live in Texas). It is done in such a nice way that they won't be offended if I tell you.

Two Texans returning from lunch stopped before the window of a Cadillac automobile agency. The first one said, "You know, I need a new Cadillac. As I recall, I haven't bought one this year."

The second Texan said, "Guess I'll join you."

They walked in, and the first Texan pointed and said, "Sign me up for two of those," and reached for his wallet. The second stopped him at once and said, "Now wait, Jim, the cars are on me. You paid for lunch."

Before you continue, think for a minute and try to guess the stereotype that's used in this joke. What have you heard about Texans? Texas is a big state with lots of oil wells and many of the people are rich. Right? And Texans like to think of themselves as big spenders. This stereotype is certainly an exaggeration, but it works well in this joke. Where else but in Texas can a man walk into an automobile agency and buy two cars as easily as he could walk into a restaurant and buy two hamburgers?

Although different comedians would probably come up with different categories of jokes, most would agree with the basic ones you've been introduced to: the anticlimax joke, the put-down, the wordplay or pun, and the ethnic joke. As you listen to the various jokes presented in the following units, I hope you'll try to classify them. Most important, I hope you enjoy and laugh at what you hear!

But before you do anything else, answer these very serious true-or-false questions.

Write your anwers here.

1. Most jokes fall in the following categories: anticlimax, put-down, wordplay or pun, and ethnic humor. _____

2. The joke about Al Jolson is an ethnic joke. _____

3. Comedians feel that stereotypes make poor butts of humor. _____

Check Yourself

Re-read the monologue before you do the exercises. When you have finished, check your answers on pages 157 and 8.

1. COMPREHENSION CHECK. Answer each question with a sentence.

1. How are the anticlimax joke and the put-down joke similar? How are they different? _____

   _____

   _____

2. In the pun about the cows, which word is used in two different ways?

_____

_____

3. What stereotype is used in the joke about the Texans? _____

_____

2. WHAT'S MISSING? Complete the jokes using words from the monologue. You may need to re-read the jokes.

When _____ young _____ director told the

_____ that he _____ do a _____ better, Mr. Jolson

_____ what _____ was _____, _____ at

_____ young _____ angrily, and _____,

"_____, kid, _____ got a _____ dollars. What

_____ you _____ ?"

The director looked _____ him and said _____,

"_____."

Follow It Up

Apply your new knowledge and use your new vocabulary by doing the exercises that follow.

1. WORKING TOGETHER. Write eight questions using new words from Part II of the Introduction.

1. _____?
2. _____?
3. _____?
4. _____?
5. _____?
6. _____?
7. _____?
8. _____?

2. FINDING SYNONYMS. For each underlined word or phrase, think of a synonym from the unit. Then use the synonym in a sentence that answers the question.

1. Can you <u>remember</u> what you did in school last Monday? _____

   _____

2. Did your brother really do something so <u>mean</u>? _____

   _____

3. Who is your favorite American <u>funny person</u>? _____

   _____

4. Do you have any <u>numbers</u> to prove your favorite ice cream is more

   popular than mine? _____

   _____

5. Which <u>part of the movie</u> did you enjoy the most? _____

   _____

3. COMPLETING SENTENCES. Fill in the blanks with words from this list. Be sure to use the correct form.

Cadillac	insult	bunch	oversimplified
agency	judge	herd	entertainer

1. How many cattle does Mr. Marcos have in his _____?

2. You _____ the problem. I'm afraid it won't be so easy to solve.

3. I can't believe you ate that whole _____ of grapes.

4. Bob Hope is one of America's best-known _____ .

5. They left the party before dinner was served. What an _____.

6. Is it difficult to park a big car like a _____?

7. I called the travel _____ and asked them to send us some information about trips to Egypt.

8. Margo Robbins thinks we _____ her unfairly. She wants another interview.

12

Take It Further

1. What are common butts of jokes in your country?
2. What subjects in your country are taboo—that is, they cannot be joked about?
3. What are common stereotypes of people in your country?
4. Have you ever had an embarrassing experience concerning jokes and American humor? Share your experience with your classmates.
5. Tell the class a joke that is popular in your country. Describe the structure of the joke, and then explain why it is funny in your country. Give your classmates the background they need to understand it. Tell them if the joke "loses something in the translation."
6. In your own words, recreate one of the jokes you read in this unit. First summarize the events of the joke, and then try to tell it for laughs—as though you are the comedian.
7. Read each of the following jokes. First identify the category it falls in, and then identify the butt of the joke, the build-up, the point where the alteration occurs, and the punch line.

    a. When I was a kid, I thought that all fairy tales began with the line "Once upon a time. . . . " Now that I'm grown-up, I know that all fairy tales begin with the line "If I'm elected. . . . "

    b. Every time he opens his mouth, he puts his feat in it.
        ("feat" means achievement. *Hint:* What word sounds exactly like "feat"?)

    c. In Chicago, elections are very interesting. On election day, all party members are told to vote early and often.
        (Chicago is known for its dishonest political parties.)

    d. Our next speaker is well known. He's been written up many times. He's got ninety-eight parking tickets.
        ("written up" means news articles or reports that are written about a person or event. Parking tickets are "written up" by police officers when cars are in a parking space too long or in a space not permitted for cars.)

    e. DOCTOR: I'm about to operate.
        INTERN: May I cut in?
        ("cut in" means interrupt.)

f.   An Irishman was brought before a judge for drunkenness.
"Where did you get the liquor?" demanded the judge.
"A Scotsman gave it to me," the Irishman replied.
"That's 30 days in jail for perjury!" said the judge.
("perjury" means not telling the truth.)

8.   According to the joke above, what do you think is a stereotype of the Irish? Of the Scots?

The Delivery

PART I

"Number 25? That's the best joke I've ever heard!"

Get Ready

Do the GET READY activities before listening to the comedian's jokes and commentary. These activities will help you understand the comedian.

1. LET'S TALK. There is more to being funny than just saying funny words. After comedians select their material, they spend hours working on their delivery (that is, their presentation). What do you think comedians should pay attention to when they practice delivering their lines?

2. BUILD YOUR VOCABULARY. Try to guess the meanings of the words in bold italics.

1. I could tell from the **inflection** in your voice that you really didn't mean what you said.

2. An information question such as "Is your name Jane?" should be spoken with rising **intonation**.

3. The speech that Jake Williams made to his employees about getting to work on time **fell flat on its face**. Nobody listened, and nobody came to work on time.

4. The **climax** of my story was when the big dog saved the little girl from the villain. It was the most exciting event in the entire story.

5. I didn't dislike what you said to me. I disliked the way you said it. Your **tone of voice** was insulting.

6. When you said, "Today you look happy," why did you **stress** the word "today"? Don't I look happy every day?

7. Your **pacing** isn't good. You're reading your speech so quickly that I can't understand what you're saying. Pause after you say something important so that I can consider what you've said.

8. Max is a real **con man**. He's always tricking people. Last week he sold me a piece of glass for $1,000 and called it a diamond.

9. When you said you loved your job, you didn't sound as though you meant it. I think you were being **sarcastic**.

10. That joke you told **bombed**. It was terrible, and nobody laughed.

11. Tell me what happened at the end of the game. Don't keep me in **suspense**. Who won?

12. I didn't say your answer was wrong in front of your mother, because I didn't want to embarrass you; I wanted you to **save face**.

13. The new restaurant Tom bought could **make or break** him. He could become rich or poor depending on how successful it is.

14. Jackie was really **burned up** when an oil truck ran into her car. I thought she was going to hit the truck driver. It took her the entire afternoon to **cool down**.

15. The **recipe** for happiness is love, good health, and success.

Here are some additional words you will need to know. Check the Glossary for any of these words you don't understand.

amazed	emphasis	mundane
bum	gambling	peals (of laughter)
catalyst	grounds (for divorce)	prank
comprise	holler	ruin (v.)
cool down	inmate	signal (v.)
digest (v.)	message	suburbs
dual	monologue	

3. PREVIEW THESE SENTENCES. Listen to the Preview Sentences for Unit One, Part I. Then fill in the missing words. You may check your answers on page 121.

1. Jack, a new _____, saw Wally, an old _____, walk up to a prisoner, call out "Number 25!" and walk away, leaving the prisoner laughing.

2. Words certainly contribute to the end result, but the _____, the _____, the _____, and everything else that _____ the delivery of a joke have the power to turn ordinary words into _____ of laughter.

3. He might deliver it without any obvious emphasis and "throw it away" as if the words were unimportant, or he might use a _____ tone of voice or an accent and be even more successful.

4. Without the right _____ and _____, the joke will _____, _____, and die!

5. It gives the audience a chance to _____ all the information they've heard; at the same time, it creates a little _____ as it _____ that the _____ is just about to come.

Make sure you understand what the sentences mean before you continue.

Now, Let's Laugh

⊙⊙ Listen to the comedian. Then decide if the statements you hear at the end of the monologue are true or false. You may check your answers on page 157.

Write your answers here.

1. There is only one way to tell a joke. _____

2. The wrong emphasis can ruin a joke. _____

3. A joke is successful when it bombs. _____

4. Audiences often laugh because they don't want to admit they didn't understand the joke. _____

Check Yourself

Listen to the comedian again before you do the exercises. When you have finished, check your answers on pages 157 and 122.

1. COMPREHENSION CHECK. Answer each question with a sentence.

1. What are some of the things that contribute to the delivery? _____

    _____

2. What are the different ways a comedian can deliver a line? _____

    _____

3. Why is the pause before the punch line important? _____

    _____

4. Why was the husband who was driving with his wife amazed? _____

    _____

2. WHAT'S MISSING? Listen again, and complete the jokes with the missing words or phrases.

"I can't _____ him for _____ minute," Ethel

_____. "He gets _____, spends all our _____ on

_____ and other women, and if he comes home at all, it's just to

change clothes."

"It _____ looks like you have _____," the

lawyer said.

"Divorce?" Ethel hollered. "I _____ say not! _____

lived with that _____ for thirty years. _____ I should

make him _____?"

"Mommy," said the _____ boy. "Are you still _____

about my _____?"

"Well," she said, "I guess I've _____ a bit."

"Well," he said, "you're gonna get _____ again. . . . I just

_____ the living room on _____."

Follow It Up

Apply your new knowledge and use your new vocabulary by doing the exercises that follow.

1. WORKING TOGETHER. In pairs, write a summary of what you heard in this part of Unit One. Use as many of the new words and expressions as you can.

_____

_____

_____

_____

_____

_____

_____

_____

_____

_____

_____

2. FINDING SYNONYMS. Write a word or expression from this unit that is similar in meaning to the underlined words.

1. The highest point of the play was very exciting. _____

2. I was quite surprised when I saw your little sister driving that truck.

_____

3. There was a lesson in that story. _____

4. Why are you wasting your time betting money on card games? _____

_____

5. That singer will fail badly if she doesn't get rid of her cold. _____

_____

6. That man who is always tricking you belongs in jail. _____

7. Why did you yell at your brother? _____

8. On Halloween, children play tricks on their friends. _____

3. COMPLETING SENTENCES. Fill in the blanks with words from this list. Be sure to use the correct form.

recipe   suspense   grounds for divorce   message
sarcastic   digest   fall flat on its face   burned up
emphasis   comprise   peals of laughter   signal
dual   suburbs   save face

1. I am not being _____. I really meant it when I said that you did a good job.

2. Don't keep me in _____! Please tell me what happened at the meeting.

3. When nobody laughed, I knew my joke _____.

4. After I finish my work in the city, I enjoy driving home to the _____.

5. Do you have a good _____ for pizza?

6. This radio serves a _____ purpose. It tells time as well as plays music.

7. If you don't do your homework every night, you'll be sorry. Do you get my _____?

8. In Japan, people are careful to help others _____.

9. Mary's husband left her and their children two years ago. She certainly has _____.

10. The money you gave me _____ only half of the money you owe. Where's the other half?

11. I can see that you're _____ about something I said. I know I hurt you, and I apologize.

12. When Mrs. Johnson raised her voice for extra _____, I knew she was angry.

13. I can't make a decision until you give me time to _____ everything you told me.

14. Chest pains may _____ that a person is going to have a heart attack.

15. I knew the children were telling each other jokes when I heard _____ from their bedroom.

PART II

"You may not be fast, but you're lovable!"

Get Ready

1. BUILD YOUR VOCABULARY. Try to guess the meanings of the words in bold italics.

1. Judging from the ***frequency*** of your trips to the zoo, you must really love animals.
2. Susan asked the stranger for help, but it was ***in vain***. He got into his car and left her.
3. The heat today is ***unbearable***. I can't sit outside another minute.
4. This dinner is a ***social function*** arranged for you to meet and talk to people.
5. You ***mimic*** your father very well. You sound just like him.
6. Our spaceship will ***orbit*** the moon twice before we return to earth.
7. No one can decide your ***fate***: whether you live or die is up to God.
8. The ***jockey*** who rode my horse in the last race knows how to handle horses well.
9. Robert speaks and acts as though he were the only important person here. He really is ***pompous***.
10. Winning your high school spelling contest was a difficult ***feat***. You can be very proud of yourself.
11. If you knew ***your number was up*** and you were going to die tomorrow, what would you do today?

12. You have a **philosophical** way of looking at life. I wish I could be as calm and patient as you.

13. Your **indifference** toward your father surprises me. Don't you love him?

14. My poor test grade doesn't **reflect** how much I know about this subject. I know a great deal, but I was very tired when I took the test.

15. My life is so dull and **mundane**. Every day I do the same things.

Here are some additional words you will need to know. Check the Glossary for any of these words you don't understand.

affectionate	mutter	second lieutenant
disgust	nonchalant	slop
genius	portion	stern
indignant/indignities	revolution	unimpressed
minimize	romantic	windbag

⊗⊗ **2. PREVIEW THESE SENTENCES.** Listen to the Preview Sentences for Unit One, Part II. Then fill in the missing words. You may check your answers on page 123.

1. Pacing is the speed at which one speaks and the length and

   _____ of pauses separating units of thought.

2. The horse hugged the rail, the _____ had his hands around

   the horse's neck, and I . . . kissed my money goodbye.

3. A young _____, listening with _____,

   _____ to the woman at his side, "What a _____ and

   _____ old _____ he is!"

4. It was in early 1962, on the day John Glenn became the first American

   to go into _____, and the nation went wild over his

   _____ of remaining in outer space for three _____.

5. The words count, but the delivery determines the _____ of the

   joke.

Make sure you understand what the sentences mean before you continue.

Now, Let's Laugh

Listen to the comedian. Then decide if the statements you hear at the end of the monologue are true or false. You may check your answers on page 157.

Write your answers here.

1. The man kissed his money because his horse won the race. _____

2. The lieutenant didn't realize he was talking to the general's wife.

   _____

3. Both Sara and Becky were excited over John Glenn's achievement.

   _____

4. Fox stayed at home because his wife was sick. _____

Check Yourself

Listen to the comedian again before you do the exercises. When you have finished, check your answers on pages 157 and 124.

1. COMPREHENSION CHECK. Answer each question with a sentence.

1. What is pacing? _____

   _____

   _____

2. Why did Fox call his office? _____

   _____

3. Why was the horse race called an "affectionate race"? _____

   _____

   _____

4. What kind (category) of joke is the one about John Glenn? _____

   _____

5. Why wouldn't Jones travel by plane? _____

   _____

2. WHAT'S MISSING? Listen again, and complete the jokes with the missing words or phrases.

It _____ in early _____, on the day John Glenn

_____ the _____ American to go into _____, and

the _____ went wild over his _____ of remaining in

_____ space for three _____. The _____ day, Sara,

still _____, said to her _____ Becky, "_____ do you

_____ of John Glenn?"

Becky _____ her eyebrows and said, "_____?"

Sara, astonished at _____ lack of _____, said, "John

Glenn! John Glenn! He just _____ around the _____

three _____!"

Becky shrugged her _____. "Well," she said, "if you have

_____, you can afford to _____."

For years, Jones _____ refused to take planes, and all

arguments urging _____ to do so were made _____.

Finally one _____ said in _____, "Listen,

_____, why don't you take a _____ approach?

Tell _____ that if your _____ isn't up, then it isn't up, and

_____ the plane."

"Ah," said _____, "and what _____ would it

_____ if my _____ wasn't up, but the _____

number was?"

Follow It Up

Apply your new knowledge and use your new vocabulary by doing the exercises that follow.

1. WORKING TOGETHER. In pairs, write a dialog or short story using at least ten of the words or expressions that appear in Part II of this unit. (It doesn't have to be funny.)

_____

_____

_____
_____
_____
_____
_____

2. FINDING SYNONYMS. Write a word or expression from this unit that is similar in meaning to the underlined words.

1. The person riding the horse is wearing red and blue. _____

2. Landing on the moon was a wonderful achievement. _____

3. Einstein was a brilliant person. _____

4. She likes to imitate her teacher's way of speaking. _____

5. We have several dinners and parties to attend this month. _____

6. Don't understate the importance of your success. We all know you're wealthy and famous. _____

7. Do you lead an ordinary life or an exciting one? _____

3. COMPLETING SENTENCES. Fill in the blanks with words from this list. Be sure to use the correct form.

in vain	indignant	affectionate	disgust
fate	pompous	unbearable	lieutenant
reflect	nonchalant	philosophical	portion

1. We always seem to meet each other in strange places. It must be

   _____.

2. You're lucky to have such _____ children who hug you often.

3. After waiting for a train that never came, Paul left the station in

   _____.

4. Max Tyler always talks at great length about his many achievements.
   He is such a _____ windbag.

5. After I became a _____ in the army, I decided to get married.

6. The heat in the summer is _____ here. I'm thinking about
   moving.

7. I'm on a diet, so please give me a very small _____ of your
   delicious-looking dessert.

8. I was surprised at your _____ behavior when you went up for your award. You acted as if you didn't care.

9. I tried very hard to prevent Jack from moving to California, but my efforts were _____. He moved last week.

10. It's hard to be _____ when you're about to go to jail for a crime you didn't commit.

11. You got what you deserved. Don't be so _____!

12. This gift _____ my feelings for you.

Take It Further

1. Choose one of the jokes from this unit, and recreate it in your own words.
2. Comedians aren't the only people who have to pay attention to their delivery. What other people are concerned with the various elements of the presentation (delivery)?
3. Discuss the two basic intonation patterns in English (rising-falling and rising) with your teacher. For what kinds of sentences do you use them? Describe the patterns for the sentences below. You may even diagram them.
   a. Are you doing your homework now?
   b. What a beautiful day!
   c. How do you feel this morning?
   d. You bought a new car, didn't you?
   e. This is your book, isn't it?
   f. So, you're moving soon?
   g. Are you going to eat lunch in school or at home?
   h. I suggest you read this terrific book.
4. Look at the joke that follows. Read it to yourself silently, underline the words that should be stressed, mark the places where you should pause, and indicate the intonation pattern (rising-falling or rising). Practice the joke a few times, and then read it aloud—if possible, for laughs. You may work on this activity in pairs after you work on it yourself.

> The indignant soldier was writing a furious letter to his Congressman, detailing all the various indignities and evils he was suffering.
>
> "And the food, sir," he wrote, "can only be described as slop. I wouldn't feed it to pigs for fear they would get sick to their stomachs and die from it. It would be rejected by any decent garbage man. And to make matters worse, they serve such small portions."

Introducing . . .
The Professions!

PART I

"I can't fix the leak. Why not make it a swimming pool?"

Get Ready

Do the GET READY activities before listening to the comedian's jokes and commentary. These activities will help you understand the comedian.

1. LET'S TALK.   For a variety of reasons, joking about our jobs and the way they are performed is very common in America.   What are these reasons?   Discuss why people joke in general and why jokes about professions are popular.

2. BUILD YOUR VOCABULARY.   Try to guess the meanings of the words in bold italics.

1.   The man who fixed my computer is *inept*.   He didn't know what he was doing.
2.   After my brother broke my watch, I *paid* him *back* by breaking his watch.
3.   Computers store messages *electronically*.
4.   You are so lucky to have a good job.   I *envy* you and wish I had one like yours.
5.   Whenever I eat hot or spicy food, my stomach feels sick.   I get *indigestion*.
6.   Doctor, can you *prescribe* something that will help me get rid of my indigestion?
7.   The kitchen sink must be *clogged up* with something.   The water won't go down.
8.   Paul got sick when he took an *overdose* of medicine.   He was supposed to take only two pills a day, but instead he took five.
9.   This is the same kind of work I do every day.   It's *routine* work.
10.   He likes to *work me over* in front of my friends and get us all laughing.
11.   Why are you so *hostile*?   You act as if you could hit somebody.
12.   If you are the *witness* who saw the accident, please tell the police.

Here are some additional words you will need to know.   Check the Glossary for any of these words you don't understand.

advertise	greed	precede
appendicitis/appendix	jury	pump (v.)
aspirin	obviously	relieve
complaint	patience	retainer
entitle	plumber	trip (v.)

3. PREVIEW THESE SENTENCES. Listen to the Preview Sentences for Unit Two, Part I. Then fill in the missing words. You may check your answers on page 125.

1. In fact, we often joke about our work or about someone else's profession, in order to _____ fear and _____.

2. I called my doctor the other day and told him I had taken an _____ of _____.

3. "Relax. It couldn't possibly be _____. She probably has a touch of _____."

4. Doctors aren't the only professionals that get _____ by comedians.

5. So he found a lawyer who _____ that, for a $50 _____, he could help anybody.

Make sure you understand what the sentences mean before you continue.

Now, Let's Laugh

⊙ ⊙ Listen to the comedian. Then decide if the statements you hear at the end of the monologue are true or false. You may check your answers on page 158.

Write your answers here.

1. People never joke about their own work, only about other people's work. _____

2. It's possible to keep people alive electronically. _____

3. Mr. Jones called his doctor because his wife had indigestion. _____

4. People fear and envy lawyers. _____

5. The joke about Harry and his lawyer shows the greed of business-people. _____

Check Yourself

Listen to the comedian again before you do the exercises. When you have finished, check your answers on pages 158, 125, and 126.

1. COMPREHENSION CHECK. Answer each question with a sentence.

1. Which joke is an example of a "put-down" joke? _____

   _____

2. What happened to the patient who was kept alive by machines when the nurse tripped over the wires and pulled out the plugs? _____

   _____

3. How did the plumber pay his doctor back? _____

   _____

4. How do some doctors respond to patients' complaints? _____

   _____

2. WHAT'S MISSING? Listen again, and complete the jokes with the missing words.

I called my _____ the other _____ and _____ him I had _____ an _____ of _____. I said, "What _____ _____ _____?" He said, "Take _____ aspirin and _____ me _____ _____ morning."

Mr. Jones hadn't _____ his _____ for _____ _____. Now it was two o'clock in the _____, and his _____ had a bad _____ that he was sure was _____. The _____ said, "_____. It couldn't _____ be appendicitis. She _____ has a touch of _____. I took out your _____ appendix _____ years _____, and in all of _____ history, I've _____ heard of _____ having a _____ appendix."

"That may be _____," Mr. _____ said, "but _____ you ever _____ of anybody having a _____ wife?"

30

Follow It Up

Apply your new knowledge and use your new vocabulary by doing the exercises that follow.

1. WORKING TOGETHER. In pairs, write a dialog or short story using at least ten of the words and expressions that appear in this part of Unit Two.

_____

_____

_____

_____

_____

_____

_____

_____

_____

_____

_____

_____

_____

2. FINDING SYNONYMS. Write a word or expression from this unit that is similar in meaning to the underlined words.

1. The man who came to fix my kitchen sink did a good job. _____

2. I got sick from taking too many pills. _____.

3. The person who saw the accident is only ten years old. _____

4. Who went ahead of Roger? _____

5. The twelve people in court who will decide whether Rick is guilty will probably have a hard time making a decision. _____

6. Jack took two pills for headaches. _____

7. Did you get a sick stomach from that pizza? _____

3. COMPLETING SENTENCES. Fill in the blanks with words from this list. Be sure to use the correct form.

electronically	complaint	patience	routine
inept	clogged up	pay back	
envy	prescribe	entitle	

1. I wish I had a home like yours. I _____ you.

2. Nothing will go down this pipe because it's _____.

3. This machine runs _____.

4. Don't get angry at the children today. Try not to lose your

   _____.

5. I see my doctor every year for a _____ examination.

6. The man who worked on my car is _____. He didn't correct

   the problem; in fact, he made it worse.

7. You don't seem to be satisfied with the car you bought. What's your

   _____?

8. What did the doctor _____ for the red spots on your face?

9. This paper _____ you to a seven-day vacation. All you have

   to do is sign it.

10. Last week I _____ my girlfriend. I made her cry for leaving

    me.

"A fly in your soup? That's all right, sir; he won't eat much."

Get Ready

1. BUILD YOUR VOCABULARY. Try to guess the meanings of the words in bold italics.

1. Everybody in this class must do the homework assignment; nobody is ***exempt***.
2. The roast beef is ***smothered in gravy***. It's so thick that I can't taste the meat.
3. I was ***infuriated*** when I heard I missed my plane by one minute.
4. Ronald Brown deserves ***recognition*** for saving two children from a burning house. Everybody should know what a brave thing he did.
5. I'm a little ***hard-pressed*** for money now, so I can't buy the car I wanted.

6. When you said we would probably be the only people on the plane, I didn't believe you. Now I see you meant it **literally**. We are alone.
7. I'll always remember how Susan **befriended** me in the airport when I discovered I had lost my passport.
8. Here's my **proposition**: If you leave town today, I'll give you $5,000.
9. My dentist **gives me the gas** so that I'll be asleep and feel no pain while he's working on my teeth.
10. Don't be so **boisterous**. I can understand you better if you aren't so loud and noisy.

Here are some additional words you will need to know. Check the Glossary for any of these words you don't understand.

calculating	optometrist	sacred
cheap person	realtor	wizard
nap	retired	

⚙⚙ **2. PREVIEW THESE SENTENCES.** Listen to the Preview Sentence for Unit Two, Part II. Then fill in the missing words. You may check your answers on page 126.

1. The phone rang at the firehouse just five minutes after the men had all _____ for their afternoon _____.

2. Not even movie stars are _____ from jokes.

3. Here's one about a waiter who doesn't really know much about food preparation and takes his orders too _____.

4. I'm counting my money before you _____.

5. So he went to see a man he'd once _____—Bob Baker, the _____—about renting a cheap building.

Make sure you understand what the sentences mean before you continue.

34

Now, Let's Laugh

⚙⚙ Listen to the comedian. At the end of the monologue, you will hear the first half of four different statements. Decide which of the endings logically completes each statement. You may check your answers on page 158.

Write the number of the correct ending next to the appropriate statement.

1. didn't trust his dentist

2. buy a butcher shop

3. was a cheap person

4. needed his eyes checked

5. was smothered in gravy

a. A man went to see an optometrist because he _____.

b. The police officer's advice to the movie actor was to _____.

c. In the joke about the dentist, the patient _____.

d. Max, a businessman, raised his offer because Bob _____.

Check Yourself

⚙⚙ Listen to the comedian again before you do the exercises. When you have finished, check your answers on pages 158 and 127.

1. COMPREHENSION CHECK. Answer each question with a sentence.

1. Why does the waiter respond so angrily to his customer in the joke about the "chicken smothered in gravy"? _____

_____

2. What did the homeowner do while he was waiting for the plumber?

_____

3. Why did the police officer suggest that the actor buy a butcher shop?

_____

4. Why did Max go to see Bob Baker about renting a cheap building?

_____

2. WHAT'S MISSING? Listen again, and complete the jokes with the missing words.

The _____ rang at the _____ just _____ minutes _____ the men had all _____ for their _____ nap. "_____ was a _____ blast at my _____," a woman _____. "The _____ are _____ through the _____ and the first _____. _____ soon _____ destroy the _____ place."

"_____ you try _____ water over it?" _____ the fire _____.

"Yes!" _____ the woman.

"Then _____ no use _____ our _____ over. _____ all we _____."

The _____ movie _____ stopped the _____ _____ and asked for _____. Then he _____ for some _____ of _____, but none came. "Er-uh, don't you _____ me?" he _____ the cop.

"Sure, you're the _____ who's gonna buy that _____ shop on Seventh Avenue."

"No, no," said the _____. "_____ you seen me in _____?"

"Yes. And _____ my _____. _____ that _____ shop."

Follow It Up

Apply your new knowledge and use your new vocabulary by doing the exercises that follow.

1. WORKING TOGETHER. In pairs, write a dialog or short story using at least ten words or expressions that appear in Part II of this unit. (It doesn't have to be funny.)

_____

_____

_____

_____

_____

_____

_____

_____

2. FINDING SYNONYMS. Write a word or expression from this unit that is similar in meaning to the underlined words.

1. You are not <u>excused</u> from paying taxes. Everyone must pay them.

   _____

2. This is a very <u>noisy</u> crowd. _____

3. Because I can't get a loan, I feel <u>pushed into a corner</u>. _____

4. Did you go to an <u>eye doctor</u> yet? _____

5. Will you accept my <u>offer</u> of $5,000 for your car? _____

3. COMPLETING SENTENCES. Fill in the blanks with words from this list. Be sure to use the correct form.

calculating	give me the gas	befriend	nap
realtor	wizard	retire	
recognition	smothered in gravy	sacred	

1. Please don't work on my teeth until you _____.

2. After he _____ from his job, he had nothing to do.

3. I'd like my steak _____.

4. Terry Kent has invented so many things. She's a true _____.

5. Paul _____ me when I was just ten years old, and we've been good friends ever since.

6.   I'll have more energy after I take my _____.

7.   I don't want to appear so _____, but I must make sure I'm not paying you too much for your service.

8.   Be quiet as you enter this church. This is a _____ place for many people.

9.   The _____ has sold over a thousand homes.

10. Diane Keaton, the actress, deserves _____ for her wonderful performance in this movie.

Take It Further

1.   Recreate one of the jokes you heard in this unit. First tell it in your own words, and then tell it for laughs.
2.   Are jokes about professions popular in your country? Are any professions too sacred or controversial to be the subject of humor? Explain.
3.   If you know any good jokes about specific professions, share them with the class.
4.   Which professions are most respected in your country? Explain why. (Consider education, social status, and salary.) Which are considered the least desirable occupations? Explain why.
5.   Do you agree with the thoughts and feelings expressed in the jokes you heard about doctors and lawyers? Explain. Do people in your country feel this way about these professionals?
6.   Read the following joke, and then answer the questions.

> NEWCOMER AT THE GATES OF HEAVEN: Knock, knock.
> WELCOMING ANGEL: Who is it?
> NEWCOMER: It is I.
> WELCOMING ANGEL: Oh, no! Not another damn English teacher!

a.   How did the angel know the newcomer was an English teacher?
b.   Why did the angel react negatively?
c.   What is this joke telling us about the stereotype of the English teacher?

Government and Politics

PART I

"If you're going to talk politics, I'm leaving."

Get Ready

Do the GET READY activities before listening to the comedian's jokes and commentary. These activities will help you understand the comedian.

1. LET'S TALK. No matter what country you visit, the people there are likely to discuss government affairs. What may differ from country to country is how much criticism of government leaders and activities you will hear. What do you think goes on in America? Can people openly criticize their government? Do Americans joke about their leaders and their decisions and affairs?

2. BUILD YOUR VOCABULARY. Try to guess the meanings of the words in bold italics.

1. Are famous people *fair game* for reporters who constantly wait for them to do something of interest to the public?

2. Jack Daniels isn't doing a good job of *impersonating* Mr. Reagan. His voice doesn't sound at all like the president's.

3. Since you are not my boss, I am not *accountable* to you. I don't have to tell you what I'm doing all the time.

4. Prince Charles and Princess Diana are always in the *limelight*; they're in the news almost every day.

5. Presidential candidates get a lot of *media coverage*. Television, radio, newspapers, and magazines have many stories about them.

6. The President of the United States gets his advice on legal matters from the *attorney general*, the most powerful lawyer in the United States.

7. I can *visualize* what my daughter will look like at age 10, but I can't picture what she'll look like at age 20.

8. *Madison Square Garden* is a great place for the circus or a college graduation or any big event, because there are seats for a very large audience.

9. Although we have been *foes* for many years, I hope it's possible for us to forget our differences and become friends after the election.

10. Mr. Marchand and I are *adversaries*. We're running against each other in our city's election.

11. When President Richard Nixon announced that he was resigning the presidency, reporters had a *field day*. They had an exciting time reporting stories about Mr. Nixon.

12. What was that *crack* you made about my hair? Don't make fun of it!

13. Paul Wyman is a *self-made* man. Without any help from friends or family, he created a very successful company.

14. Representatives from all over the world meet at the *United Nations headquarters* in New York City to discuss world peace.

15. Abraham Lincoln was *assassinated* by someone who hated him and what he stood for.

Here are some additional words you will need to know. Check the Glossary for any of these words you don't understand.

appoint	fire (v.)	retire
assault (n.)	genuine	roman numerals
bureaucrat	hire	strategy
compliment	impressionist	structure
communicator	incompetent	term
criticize/criticism	keen	weapon
donate	mechanics	wit

⊙⊙ **3. PREVIEW THESE SENTENCES.** Listen to the Preview Sentences for Unit Three, Part I. Then fill in the missing words. You may check your answers on page 128.

1. Government leaders and politicians on all levels of government—local, state, and national—are _____ for comedians.

2. And even if we are not directly involved in the everyday _____ of running our government, we have directly voted for the people who are.

3. Politicians are more likely to listen to humorous _____ than to bitter verbal _____.

4. President Ronald Reagan, considered by friends and _____ alike to be an excellent _____, also used humor to its best advantage, especially during his last presidential campaign.

5. It is a program that was adopted in 1935 to ensure that _____ Americans would have money to live on.

6. In order to appreciate this joke, you have to know that children in America usually get at least one set of building blocks during their childhood and have great fun building different _____.

Make sure you understand what the sentences mean before you continue.

Now, Let's Laugh

⚙ ⚙ Listen to the comedian. Then decide if the statements you hear at the end of the monologue are true or false. You may check your answers on page 158.

Write your answers here.

1. Speaking out against the government is expected in the United States.

    _____

2. Politicians are more likely to listen to verbal assaults than to

    humorous criticism. _____

3. Johnny Carson is the host of a popular television show. _____

4. President Reagan got angry when people told jokes about his age.

    _____

5. Mr. Rockefeller got the United Nations headquarters for Christmas.

    _____

Check Yourself

⚙ ⚙ Listen to the comedian again before you do the exercises. When you have finished, check your answers on pages 158, 129, and 131.

1. COMPREHENSION CHECK. Answer each question with a sentence.

1. Give at least one reason why comedians concentrate much of their

    attention on what politicians are doing and not doing. _____

    _____

2. Who are regular butts of humor on Johnny Carson's nightly show?

    _____

3. Why did President John F. Kennedy respond humorously to the

    reporters' questions about appointing Bobby Kennedy attorney

    general? _____

4. Why are politicians the object of continuous media coverage? _____

    _____

5. Why did Lyndon Johnson ask Joey Adams for a big introduction before

    he delivered a speech at Madison Square Garden? _____

    _____

2. WHAT'S MISSING? Listen again, and complete the jokes with the missing words.

When a _____ asked John F. Kennedy, _____ President of the _____ _____, how he could _____ his young _____, Bobby Kennedy, _____ was just out of _____ school, as the _____ _____ of the most _____ country in the world, _____ smiled and said, "Well, _____ my _____ brother, and I _____ to give him some _____ before he _____ his own law _____."

I _____ him at _____ _____ _____ one night as the _____ President in the _____ of our _____. _____ said, "My _____ would have _____ that _____, and my mother would have _____ it. It's the _____ introduction I ever got. _____ one time in _____, the _____ was supposed to _____ me and he _____ make it, so I _____ myself."

Follow It Up

Apply your new knowledge and use your new vocabulary by doing the exercises that follow.

1. WORKING TOGETHER. Work in pairs. Select sixteen words and expressions from those introduced in this part of Unit Three. Using these words, create questions that show your understanding of them. Then ask your partner your questions, and together evaluate your responses.

_____

_____

_____

_____

_____

_____

_____

_____

2. FINDING SYNONYMS. Write a word or expression from this unit that is similar in meaning to the underlined words.

1. I didn't like your joke about my short mother. _____

2. I am directly involved in the operations of this company. _____

3. I don't like to eat and drink with my enemies. _____

4. Is Sally Richards pretending to be the president's wife? _____

5. It's hard to picture you as a child. _____

6. Did you buy a real diamond ring? _____

7. Do you think your uncle will ever recover from that violent attack he experienced last month? _____

8. Most celebrities seem to enjoy the attention they get from television and newspapers. _____

9. I was named for this position; I didn't ask for it. _____

10. Most people like the President's ability to make clever remarks. _____

_____

3. COMPLETING SENTENCES. Fill in the blanks with words from this list. Be sure to use the correct form.

donate	structure	field day	retire
bureaucrat	impressionist	fair game	hire
adversary	criticize	term	attorney general
roman numerals	keen	compliment	

1. The reporters had a _____ with the wedding of the Prince of England.

2. Who _____ the money for the new public square?

3. Robert has a _____ sense of humor.

4. Who is the _____ of New York State?

5. I, II, III, and IV are examples of _____.

6. What is the tallest _____ in your country?

7. I don't mind an _____ making fun of me if he or she does a good job.

8. Is this your first or second _____ as a New York senator?

9. Why did you _____ from your job before your 62nd birthday?

10. Do you think children should be considered _____ for reporters?

11. Government _____ are sometimes hard to deal with.

12. We haven't always been _____. We used to be friends.

13. Please don't _____ me in front of the children. If you have to say something nasty to me, wait until later.

14. Which person did you _____ for the job?

15. Thank you for that lovely _____. I'm glad you like my work.

"When I listen to them, I'm thankful only one of them can get elected."

Get Ready

1. BUILD YOUR VOCABULARY. Try to guess the meaning of the words in bold italics.

1. The president of that publishing company **wields** a lot of power. When he speaks, people listen.
2. After **embezzling** $10,000 from me, my secretary quit her job and left the country.
3. Baby Doc's rule of Haiti was not known for excellence. Quite the opposite: It brought him into **disgrace**.
4. The Simon family **made a mint** when they sold their ten-bedroom house.
5. There was such **chaos** at our home the day we started moving. Everything was out of place, and nobody seemed to know what to do.

6. Buying a car when you don't have a job is very **risky business.**
7. Larry isn't **eligible** for marriage because he's already married.
8. You've told me many things about your new coat, but you still haven't answered my question. Now, will you please give me a **straight answer** and tell me how much it cost?
9. It was sad to see such an important world leader **fall from power.** I wonder how he'll adjust to being an ordinary citizen.
10. Most Americans found it hard to believe that so many government officials were involved in the **Watergate scandal.**

Here are some additional words you will need to know. Check the Glossary for any of these words you don't understand.

abuse (v.)	publicity	shame (v.)
interpret	reflect	spotlight
old-timer	sensational	trustworthy
physician	sensitive	

◎ ◎ **2. PREVIEW THESE SENTENCES.** Listen to the Preview Sentences for Unit Three, Part II. Then fill in the missing words. You may check your answers on page 131.

1. We can't help but admire, envy, and often respect people who are in the _____ and _____ power.

2. The media may ignore the good ones and tell us only about the ones who lie, cheat, and _____.

3. It is very _____ to ask a woman her age.

4. A sidewalk interviewer asked one of our _____ what he thought of the two candidates for the election.

5. "The Bible tells how the world was created out of _____, and how could there by any order brought out of _____ without an engineer?"

Make sure you understand what the sentences mean before you continue.

Now, Let's Laugh

⊕ ⊕   Listen to the comedian. Then decide if the statements you hear at the end of the monologue are true or false. You may check your answers on page 158.

Write your answers here.

1. Politicians who have fallen from power never make any money. _____

2. When you ask an American woman her age, she probably won't give you a straight answer. _____

3. In the joke about the candidate who was elected and called his wife, the word that the husband and wife used differently was "honestly."

   _____

4. To be President of the United States, you must be at least 35 years old. _____

Check Yourself

⊕ ⊕   Listen to the comedian again before you do the exercises. When you have finished, check your answers on pages 158 and 132.

1. COMPREHENSION CHECK. Answer each question with a sentence.

1. The joke about politicians who disgrace themselves and write books is an example of what kind of joke—ethnic, word play, or anticlimax?

   _____

2. Why is it difficult for politicians to be honest? _____

   _____

3. According to the joke, why is it unlikely that a woman will ever be elected President? _____

4. Remember the joke about the doctor, engineer, and the politician? What is this joke really saying about politicians? _____

   _____

48

2. WHAT'S MISSING? Listen again, and complete the jokes with the missing words.

"I've been _____ ," the successful _____ excitedly _____ his wife.

"_____?" replied the _____.

"Now, why _____ into _____?"

A sidewalk _____ asked one of our _____ what he _____ of the two candidates for _____.

"When I look at them," he said _____, "I'm _____ only one of _____ can get _____."

During his _____, a politician _____ an elderly woman in the _____ who appeared _____ interested in what he said. _____, he took _____ to meet her and ask for her _____.

"Well, sir," the old _____ said, _____ him in the _____, "you're my _____ _____."

The _____ thanked her and asked _____ ," And who is your first _____?"

"Oh," she _____," just about _____."

Follow It Up

Apply your new knowledge and use your new vocabulary by doing the exercises that follow.

1. WORKING TOGETHER. In pairs, write a summary of what you heard in Part II of this unit. Use as many of the new words and expressions as you can.

_____

_____

_____

_____

_____

_____

_____

_____

_____

_____

_____

_____

_____

_____

_____

2. FINDING SYNONYMS. Write a word or expression from this unit that is similar in meaning to the underlined words.

1. You're a reliable and responsible person. _____

2. Is Mary Evans qualified to be a police officer? _____

3. When I grow up, I want to be a doctor. _____

4. Her skin is easily hurt. _____

5. I believe one of my employees is stealing my money. _____

3. COMPLETING SENTENCES. Fill in the blanks with words from this list. Be sure to use the correct form.

sensational	chaos	abuse
old-timer	shame	interpret
make a mint	reflect	fall from power

1. What did you do with your life after your _____?

2. Does your child's behavior in school _____ what she learned at home?

3. I thought you were happy here, but I was wrong. I _____ your behavior incorrectly.

4. You _____ your family when you robbed that supermarket.

5. You have no right to take company equipment home. You are
_____ your position.

6. What a _____ day for a picnic! The sun is shining brightly,
yet it isn't too hot.

7. Don't think that just because I'm an _____ I don't know what
it's like to fall in love. I was young once.

8. I _____ after my third book was published. The public
really liked it.

9. There's always such _____ in our kitchen Thanksgiving day.
Everybody is busy cooking his or her favorite dish.

Take It Further

1. Recreate one of the jokes you heard in this unit. Either tell it in your
own words as a story, or tell it as a joke.
2. Do people in your country tell jokes about the government? Explain.
3. Do you think it is proper to tell jokes about your country's government
and your leaders? Explain.
4. A famous British writer, George Bernard Shaw, said, "If you want to
tell people the truth, you'd better make them laugh first, or they'll kill
you." How does this statement apply to what you've heard in this unit
on government and politics? Do you agree with this statement?
5. Read this joke about Abraham Lincoln, and explain the punch line.

> The first time Abraham Lincoln ran for president, his
> opponent was Stephen Douglas, a very short, broad man. In
> one debate, he mentioned the fact that Douglas's father had
> been a cooper—a maker of barrels. "I am certain also that
> he was a very good one," he said, and here he paused to bow
> to Douglas, "for he has made one of the best whiskey casks I
> have ever seen."

(A "cask" is a container resembling a barrel but larger and stronger.)
6. Read the following joke about George Washington, and explain the
punch line.

> I don't know what kind of a guy George was, but I know he
> was the only Chief of State who didn't blame the previous
> administration for all his troubles.

7. What's funny about the following joke?

> Every politician claims he understands the questions of the
> day. Now if we could find one who understands the answers.

8. Fill in any name you'd like in this next joke to make it funny. Then explain it.

   _____ has promised to help all the poor people.

   That's good, because if you vote for him, by next year we'll all be poor.

9. Below is a political cartoon. Such cartoons can be found in most newspapers and in various kinds of magazines. First explain the use of such cartoons. Then explain what is happening in this one; you will need to know something about President Ronald Reagan and his Vice-President, George Bush. Study the chart on the doctor's wall carefully, for you will find something amusing (and also, a misspelling). If you are very creative, create your own political cartoon with a partner.

Reprinted with permission of Dwayne Powell, *Raleigh News & Observer*.
Copyright © 1986, Los Angeles Times Syndicate.

Members of the Family

PART I

"Who really brought my little brother—the birds and the bees, or the stork?"

Get Ready

Do the GET READY activities before listening to the comedian's jokes and commentary. These activities will help you understand the comedian.

1. LET'S TALK. No matter what country you come from, there is something you and your classmates have in common: families. Whether your families are large or small, *nuclear* or extended, they consist of relatives, and some of these relatives are possibly either the butts of humor or the family "clowns." Who are the relatives you like to talk about, and who are the ones that either tell the jokes or listen to them? Share this information with your class or group.

2. BUILD YOUR VOCABULARY. Try to guess the meanings of the words in bold italics.

1. Although most of the representatives didn't bring their *spouses* to the national conference, Bob Miller brought his wife, and Jane Halloway brought her husband.
2. Older, unmarried women use to be referred to as *spinsters*, but now we know them as independent single women.
3. I *naively* expected the president of our company, which employs over a thousand people, to remember my name.
4. Different cultures have different *codes of etiquette*. Certain behavior that is acceptable in my country may not be acceptable in yours.
5. "All the children with last names that begin with A, and their *respective* parents: please sit in the first row."
6. It was impolite of you to interrupt the speaker during her presentation. You committed a *faux pas*.
7. Andrew said he would never give away or throw away the *catcher's mitt* he used to catch those pitches in last year's baseball games.
8. Although seven-year-old Jackie wanted to know where and how babies were made, her parents wouldn't tell her about *the birds and the bees* until she was older.
9. Larry was a *precocious* child. He learned to read and write when he was only four.
10. There are just four people in my *nuclear* family: my parents, one brother, and me. But I have lots of aunts, uncles, and cousins.
11. I don't think Bill is doing a good job of *parenting*. He rarely sees his children and never helps them with anything.
12. Nobody can *outdo* you. You have done more things than anybody in this room.

Here are some additional words you will need to know. Check the Glossary for any of these words you don't understand.

boast	godliness	scent
cleanliness	pop/Pop	stork
day/sleep-away camp	regardless	transformer
erector set	roller skates	unemployed

3. PREVIEW THESE SENTENCES. Listen to the Preview Sentences for Unit Four, Part I. Then fill in the missing words. You may check your answers on page 133.

1. In fact, stand-up comedians—those people who literally stand up in front of audiences and tell jokes—spend at least half of their routines on their _____, children, brothers, mothers-in-law, and other interesting relatives like lazy cousins, _____ uncles, or _____ aunts.

2. One way they embarrass us is by _____ saying anything that _____ into their minds, _____ of how it sounds or whether it is appropriate.

3. The kids were _____ about their _____ fathers.

4. Well, you should know that in America, many parents are reluctant to discuss "_____"—that is, sexual relationships.

5. Yes, indeed, _____ children like Stacy often surprise their parents with their knowledge and their powers of reasoning.

Make sure you understand what the sentences mean before you continue.

Now, Let's Laugh

⊙⊙ Listen to the comedian. Then decide if the statements you hear at the end of the monologue are true or false. You may check your answers on page 158.

Write your answers here:

1. When children "spill the beans," they get dirty. _____

2. Stand-up comedians could spend at least half of their routines on their families. _____

3. Santa tells children what he'll bring them when they sit on his lap. _____

4. Many parents find it difficult to discuss "the birds and the bees" with their children. _____

5. Precocious children often ask very challenging questions. _____

Check Yourself

⊗ ⊗ Listen to the comedian again before you do the exercises. When you have finished, check your answers on pages 158–159 and 133–134.

1. COMPREHENSION CHECK. Answer each question with a sentence.

1. How do young children embarrass their parents? _____

_____

2. What is written in Santa's special book? _____

_____

3. What do some parents tell their children when they are asked about

"the birds and the bees"? _____

4. Why is Stacy precocious for an American child? _____

_____

5. Why do teenagers cause the most problems in parenting? _____

_____

2. WHAT'S MISSING? Listen again, and complete the jokes with the missing words.

The _____ were _____ about their _____

fathers. "My daddy _____ twice a week," _____ Henry.

"_____ nuttin'," said _____. "My _____ bathes

three _____ a week."

"Oh yeah?" said _____ Paul, not _____ to be

_____. "My daddy keeps _____ so _____, he never

_____ to take a _____."

Danny said, "I _____ ____ train, a gun, an _____ ____, a

_____ set, a _____ _____, a _____, a _____

_____, a transformer, a set of _____, a toy _____ with

cars and trucks, and a _____."

"Okay," _____ Santa. "_____ look in the book and

_____ if you _____ a good _____."

"Ah, never _____ looking in the _____. I'll

_____ for a pair of _____ _____."

Follow It Up

Apply your new knowledge and use your new vocabulary by doing the exercises that follow.

1. WORKING TOGETHER. First create your own family tree on a separate sheet of paper. Show it to your partner. Then describe your family members using at least ten words or expressions that appear in this part of Unit Four. (For example, "My Uncle _____ is unemployed.")

(name)

_____

_____

_____

_____

_____

_____

2. FINDING SYNONYMS. Write a word or expression from this unit that is similar in meaning to the underlined words.

1. Susie <u>innocently</u> thought babies were sold in supermarkets. _____

2. "Please don't forget to invite your <u>husbands and wives</u> to our company picnic next week." _____

3. My sister doesn't have much money now because she is <u>not working</u>.

   _____

4. Michael spent many hours working on his bicycle so that it would <u>perform better than</u> his competitors' bikes. _____

5. Those flowers in your office have a sweet <u>smell</u>. _____

6. David's little boy is very <u>advanced for his age</u>. _____

3. COMPLETING SENTENCES. Fill in the blanks with words from this list. Be sure to use the correct form.

spinster	pop	stork
code of etiquette	faux pas	regardless
transformer	boasting	respective

1. My _____ can change into a gun and a robot.

2. As soon as a good idea _____ into your head, tell me about it.

3. Neither Ron nor Beth is going away on vacation, because they don't like to leave their _____ parents.

4. Even though I'm still not married, I don't think of myself as a _____.

5. I'm going to leave my office early today, _____ of how it will look to my employees.

6. According to the American _____, it's impolite to walk away when someone is talking to you.

7. Did you know that last night a _____ brought my baby sister to the hospital?

8. I committed a _____ when I invited Gloria's old boyfriend to the party.

9. Robert is so boring because he spends most of our time together _____ about his athletic achievements.

Get Ready

1. BUILD YOUR VOCABULARY. Try to guess the meaning of the words in bold italics.

1. ***What's with*** your brother? He seems really excited.
2. A ***double standard*** still exists in the United States. Women often do not get the same respect as men in the working world.
3. Are your children ***spoiled***? Do they get whatever they want?
4. I know you're in love with Tom, but you'd better ***come out of the clouds*** and face the facts. He's really not as nice as you think.
5. My father isn't the only ***wage earner*** in our family. My mother works, too.
6. We tried to have your accident ***hushed up***, but it didn't work. We couldn't keep it a secret. Everybody knows what happened.
7. I don't have to tell you what this sentence means. Just read it; it's ***self-explanatory***.
8. After I win a million dollars, I'll ***have it made***. My life will be everything I want it to be.

9. Since Philip was arrested by the police, nobody talks about him. He's the **black sheep** of the family.

10. Allison was so angry at her parents last night, I thought she was planning to **run away**.

11. If you think you look as young as you did fifteen years ago, you had better take off your **rose-colored glasses** and see yourself as you really are.

12. I've already explained three times why I can't marry you. What do I have to do to help you **get the picture**?

13. John and I were so **disoriented** when we finally arrived in Paris, we gave the taxi driver the wrong directions and the wrong money. We didn't know what we were doing.

14. If you're going to criticize Mrs. David's clothes, please do it **subtly**. If you're too direct, you'll hurt her feelings, and she'll never shop in our store again.

15. There are so many things to do around here. Why aren't you doing something useful? You have no time for **loafing**.

Here are some additional words you will need to know. Check the Glossary for any of these words you don't understand.

angel	fiancé/fiancée	reputation
attentive	ironic	roast
bequest	look up	rogue
bowling alley	maid	scrubbing
chauffeur (v.)	misfortune	wail
chore	ne'er-do-well	will (n.)
earth at my feet	psychiatrist	women's liberation movement

😊😊 **2. PREVIEW THESE SENTENCES.** Listen to the Preview Sentences for Unit Four, Part II. Then fill in the missing words. You may check your answers on page 135.

1. She wants her daughter to _____, take off her

   _____, and evaluate her fiancé in terms of his

   qualifications as a _____.

2. This is one of the reasons for the unpleasant _____ that

   mothers-in-law share.

3. Sometimes when Mother gets into her car, she's so _____ that

   she has to think for a minute about where she's going.

4. There are many families that actually have _____ and failures who are butts of family jokes.

5. Among them was his _____ nephew, who was the _____ of the family.

Make sure you understand what the sentences mean before you continue.

Now, Let's Laugh

☺☺ Listen to the comedian. Then decide if the statements you hear at the end of the monologue are true or false. You may check your answers on page 159.

Write your answers here.

1. When Louis visits his psychiatrist twice a week, he talks about his mother. _____

2. Mothers want the same things for their daughters and daughters-in-law. _____

3. Mothers spend a lot of time driving their chauffeurs different places.

    _____

4. In jokes, fathers are treated just as badly as mothers. _____

5. Family black sheep are usually mentioned in wills. _____

Check Yourself

☺☺ Listen to the comedian again before you do the exercises. When you have finished, check your answers on pages 159, 136, and 137.

1. COMPREHENSION CHECK. Answer each question with a sentence.

1. Why is Mrs. Cohen happy about her son going to a psychiatrist? _____

    _____

2. What kinds of questions do parents ask when their daughters consider marriage? _____

    _____

3. Give an example of a double standard as described in one of the jokes.

_____

_____

4. Describe the stereotype of fathers on television shows. _____

_____

5. Why did Alan go to a will-reading? _____

2. WHAT'S MISSING? Listen again, and complete the jokes with the missing words.

Mrs. Botnick and Mrs. Gordon hadn't _____ in _____.

"Tell me," asked Mrs. Botnick, "what _____ to your son?"

"My son—what a _____!" _____ Mrs. Gordon. "He

_____ a girl _____ doesn't _____ a _____

around the _____. She can't _____, and she can't

_____ a button _____ a shirt; all she _____ is sleep

late. My _____ boy brings her _____ in bed, and all day

_____ she _____ there, _____."

"How _____," _____ Mrs. Botnick. "And what about

your _____?"

"Ah, my daughter!" exclaimed Mrs. Gordon. "She _____ a

man, an _____! He won't _____ her set _____ in

the _____. He _____ her a _____ maid and a

cook, and _____ morning he _____ her _____ in

bed! And _____ makes her _____ in bed _____

day."

"_____ have it made. _____ mothers _____

them _____. They _____ them to _____, to their

_____ homes, to the _____, _____ the

_____ _____, and to _____ lessons. I know one

_____ who wanted to _____ _____ from home, and his mother

said, "Wait, I'll _____ you."

Follow It Up

Apply your new knowledge and use your new vocabulary by doing the exercises that follow.

1. WORKING TOGETHER. In pairs, write a short story or a dialog using as many of the words or expressions from Part II of this unit as possible.

_____

_____

_____

_____

_____

_____

_____

_____

_____

_____

2. FINDING SYNONYMS. Write a word or expression from this unit that is similar in meaning to the underlined words.

1. Herbert was <u>indirectly</u> told that he lost his job because of his unfriendly personality. _____

2. I was <u>doing nothing</u> all day, and I enjoyed it. _____

3. The man I am <u>engaged to marry</u> is a soldier. _____

4. Washing that floor <u>with force</u> should improve its condition. _____

5. The <u>place where we bowl</u> each week is closed. _____

6. The <u>jobs I have to do around the house</u> should take me a few hours. _____

7. Will the <u>woman who cleans your home</u> answer the door if I get there before you do? _____

8. The <u>naughty fellows</u> who ate my apple pie will be punished. _____

3. COMPLETING SENTENCES. Fill in the blanks with words from this list. Be sure to use the correct form.

come out of the clouds   psychiatrist   black sheep   angel

have it made   double standard   misfortune   run away

put the earth at my feet   look up   hushed up   chauffeur

rose-colored glasses   bequest   disoriented

1. Every day Mrs. Megan _____ her children to school.

2. John is the _____ of the family. Nobody ever sees him.

3. I had a nurse who was so kind and gentle, she was like an

    _____.

4. After I finish my exams, I'll _____. Everything

    will be great!

5. If things don't change in this house, Robert might _____.

6. It is my _____ that I must leave this town. I hate to go.

7. Most people are _____ during the first few days at a new

    job.

8. Please _____ her number in the phone book; I don't know it.

9. Edward Marlowe didn't want anybody to know about his divorce, so

    he paid his ex-wife $10,000 to have it _____.

10. With the _____ Mrs. Jones got from her aunt, she has opened

    a small shoe store.

11. After you _____, think realistically about

    making a living as an actor.

12. Have you seen a _____ about your emotional problems?

13. Do you have a _____, Tom? Do you think your wife

    should earn less than you for doing the same work?

14. Without a decent job, how can you possibly _____?

15. He's *so* optimistic; he sees life through _____.

Take It Further

1. Choose one of the jokes from this unit, and recreate it in your own words.
2. In your country:
   a. how do parents handle questions their children ask about "the birds and the bees"?
   b. with what kinds of toys do children enjoy playing?
   c. do people have wills, and are they formally read aloud to the members of the family?
   d. do different members of the family try to live near each other or share their homes?
   e. are women's roles changing? Explain.
3. Describe some of the stereotypes of family members that are popular in your country.
4. What is the average size of a family household in your country? Why is this so?
5. *Irony* is saying one thing and meaning its opposite; many American jokes are built around irony. Is the same true of jokes in your country? If so, give an example.
6. Read the following jokes, and explain the punch lines to the class.
   a. From *Tips for Teenagers*, by Fran Leibowitz:

      (If you are) a teenager blessed with uncommonly good looks, document this state of affairs by the taking of photographs. It is the only way anyone will ever believe you in the years to come.

   b. Wrinkles are hereditary. Parents get them from their children.

   c. Cleaning your house while your kids are still growing is like shoveling the walk before it stops snowing.

   d. SMALL BOY: Could I be a preacher when I grow up?
      MOTHER: Of course you may, my dear, if you want to.
      SMALL BOY: Yes, I do. I suppose I've got to go to church all my life, anyway, and it's a lot harder to sit still than to stand up and holler.

   e. "Mother, I just took a splinter out of my hand with a pin."
      "A pin! Don't you know that's dangerous?"
      "Oh no, Mother. I used a safety pin."

f.   WILLIE: Mom, do people that lie ever go to Heaven?
MOTHER: Why, of course not, Willie.
WILLIE: Gee, I bet it's lonesome up in Heaven with only God and George Washington.
("lonesome" means lonely.)

g.   "Your mother's hair is turning gray quickly. Has something bad happened?"

"Oh no. She just didn't get to the beauty parlor last week."

Marriage, Cheating, and Divorce

PART I

"Love is a three-ring circus—engagement ring, wedding ring, and suffer-ing."

Get Ready

Do the GET READY activities before listening to the comedian's jokes and commentary. These activities will help you understand the comedian.

1. LET'S TALK. The custom of getting married is practiced in most countries. What may differ from culture to culture is how seriously the "institution" of marriage is regarded. In your country, is marriage considered a lifelong commitment? What happens if a couple is very unhappy? What will they do? Discuss the answers to these questions before you listen to an American not-so-serious response to marriage, cheating, and divorce.

2. BUILD YOUR VOCABULARY. Try to guess the meanings of the words in bold italics.

1. Don't just talk about **such and such** a change. Be specific about the changes you want.
2. It's not easy living with George because he has many **idiosyncrasies**. He never likes to go anywhere during the week, he won't answer the phone after 8:00 at night, and he never answers the door on weekends.
3. In my home, my Dad **rules the roost**. Whatever he says is the law.
4. I went to **night court** to fight my traffic ticket because I felt the policeman who gave it to me was unfair.
5. The police caught the **prowler** who was trying to get into my house while I was on vacation.
6. Do you mean to tell me that you are the thief I heard about on television? You're **notorious**; everybody is talking about you.
7. No, I don't believe in **peace at any price**. I won't say or do something I don't really mean just to end an argument.
8. Wild Willie is a famous wrestler; but when he's with his little daughter, he's as **docile** as a kitten.
9. Why are you asking me so many questions? You sure are **inquisitive** today.
10. We have a **division of labor** in our house. Each member of the family has specific things to do.

Here are some additional words you will need to know. Check the Glossary for any of these words you don't understand.

acrobat	clue	indescribable	suspicion
adopt	convenient	night court	
advent	drunk	rage (v.)	
anonymous	frantic	reliable	
client	fur	superstitious	

3. PREVIEW THESE SENTENCES. Listen to the
Preview Sentences for Unit Five, Part I. Then fill in the missing words.
You may check your answers on page 138.

1. And though some marriages may resemble a three-ring circus, with

   its _____ activity, the comparison is made in jest.

2. To help you avoid embarrassment, we're going to give you practice

   identifying the _____ of a joke by omitting, from time to time,

   our formal announcement that "the following is a joke."

3. After all, what can we expect when two different people with different

   backgrounds and _____ get together and try to live

   under the same roof, supposedly forever?

4. Then there was this _____ who was brought into

   _____ _____, having been picked up on _____ of

   being the _____ night _____.

5. It _____ far into the night, and finally she couldn't take it any

   more, so she _____ the position of _____ ___ ___ _____.

**Make sure you understand what the sentences mean before you
continue.**

Now, Let's Laugh

⊙⊙ Listen to the comedian. Then decide if the statements you hear at
the end of the monologue are true or false. You may check your
answers on page 159.

Write your answers here.

1. If a person smiles, he or she may be telling a joke. _____

2. People from certain cultures may misinterpret jokes about marriage

   and divorce. _____

3. Love can discourage people from marrying. _____

4. Only people who have bad marriages joke about marriage. _____

5. American men always rule inside the home. _____

Check Yourself

Listen to the comedian again before you do the exercises. When you have finished, check your answers on pages 159 and 139.

1. COMPREHENSION CHECK. Answer each question with a sentence.

1. In what way can a marriage resemble a three-ring circus? _____
    _____

2. What are some of the clues that suggest you are hearing a joke? _____
    _____

3. Why do some people tell negative jokes about marriage? _____
    _____

4. According to the joke, why do the Baumanns have a successful
    marriage? _____

5. In the joke about the quarrel, why wasn't the husband satisfied when
    his wife adopted the position of "peace at any price" and said that she
    was wrong? _____

2. WHAT'S MISSING? Listen again, and complete the jokes with the missing words.

"_____ like to _____ you," said the _____.
"_____ _____ always _____ back on this day
_____ the happiest _____ your life."

"Thank you," the man _____, "but _____ tomorrow
that _____ to be _____."

"Yes," _____ the lawyer, "I _____. _____ why
_____ said _____ I did."

"It's _____," he _____. "_____ of
_____. I _____ all the big _____, and my
_____ makes all _____ small, _____ decisions.
_____ decides _____ house we _____,
_____ we _____ on _____, whether the
_____ should _____ to _____ schools,

_____ I _____ change _____ job, and _____
on."

"And you, _____ Baumann? What _____ of
_____ do you _____?"

"I don't _____," he _____. " The _____
_____ haven't _____ up yet."

Follow It Up

Apply your new knowledge and use your new vocabulary by doing the
exercises that follow.

1. WORKING TOGETHER. In pairs, write a summary of
what you heard in this part of Unit Five. Use as many of the new words
or expressions as you can.

_____

_____

_____

_____

_____

2. FINDING SYNONYMS. For each underlined word or
phrase, think of a synonym from this unit. Then use the synonym in a
sentence that answers the question.

1. Are the authors of this book underlined unknown? _____

2. Can you think of someone who was famous for bad reasons? _____
   _____

3. What do you do to celebrate the beginning of the new year? _____
   _____

4. Who tells everybody what to do in your house? _____
   _____

5. What are your unusual likes and dislikes? _____

6. Why are some people against using animal skins for making clothing?
   _____

7. Do you look like your mother? _____

8. Are you Jack Cutler's customer? _____

3. COMPLETING SENTENCES. Fill in the blanks with words from this list. Be sure to use the correct form.

such and such	rage	inquisitive
suspicion	prowler	division of labor
adopt	drunk	
night court	frantic	

1. A scientist should be an _____ person.

2. I couldn't get there during the day, so I went to _____.

3. Never drive when you're _____.

4. Be quiet! I think I hear a _____ in the house.

5. He was arrested on _____ of being a murderer.

6. We finished our project quickly because we had an efficient

    _____.

7. The storm _____ for several hours.

8. We have _____ a new policy.

9. Due to the _____ activity in the office, I lost track of the time.

10. Be specific. Tell Jake that you're firing him for _____

    a reason.

"And for how long do you take this bride-to-be?"

Get Ready

1. BUILD YOUR VOCABULARY. Try to guess the meanings of the words in bold italics.

1. In the middle of the night, two men **kidnapped** Jane's little girl and ran away with her to another state.
2. Molly divorced her husband because of his **extramarital affair.** She refused to share him with another woman.
3. I didn't steal your ring. Your **accusation** that I did is ridiculous.
4. It wasn't easy for Jack to move after his wife died. He **painstakingly** packed his things, ran out of the house, and never looked back.
5. The **image** I have of you is that of a very kind and gentle person.
6. He answered the phone **drowsily** because he was sleeping when you called.
7. According to our **prenuptial** agreement, if we get a divorce, we divide everything we have in half.
8. If you pay me $2,000 in **alimony** every week until I remarry, I'll give you a divorce.
9. This discussion may seem **calculating,** but I'm a practical person. Before I decide to marry you, I would like to know how much money you have.
10. Even though you've been hurt many times by women, don't be a **cynic.** Don't think that every friendship or romance you have will turn out badly.

Here are some additional words you will need to know. Check the Glossary for any of these words you don't understand.

absurd	estate	pout
BMW	grief	prevalent
clue in	hovering	rib
decent	lousy	

☺☺ **2. PREVIEW THESE SENTENCES.** Listen to the Preview Sentences for Unit Five, Part II. Then fill in the missing words. You may check your answers on page 140.

1. "I consider that _____ wildly _____," shouted the outraged Adam.

2. There, _____ over him, was Eve _____ counting his _____.

3. According to the Bible, God created Adam, the first man, in His own _____.

4. In fact, couples are actually signing _____ agreements that state how their _____ will be divided up in the event of a divorce.

5. Divorce is so _____ in Hollywood that families often can't keep track of who belongs and who doesn't.

Make sure you understand what the sentences mean before you continue.

Now, Let's Laugh

☺☺ Listen to the comedian. Then decide if the statements you hear at the end of the monologue are true or false. You may check your answers on page 140.

Write your answers here.

1. People who have extramarital affairs cheat on their spouses. _____

2. Comedians even use the Bible as a source for jokes. _____

3. Adam was created from Eve's rib. _____

4. Wedding rings are being made thinner because there are so many divorces. _____

5. Some people sign prenuptial agreements to prevent a divorce. _____

Check Yourself

Listen to the comedian again before you do the exercises. When you have finished, check your answers on pages 159, 140, and 141.

1. COMPREHENSION CHECK. Answer each question with a sentence.

1. What is one of the causes of divorce? _____

2. Why was Eve counting Adam's ribs? _____

    _____

3. What did Morris' wife learn about Morris from all of her questions?

    _____

4. Why do people sign prenuptial agreements? _____

    _____

5. Why is it difficult for Hollywood families to keep track of who belongs in the family? _____

2. WHAT'S MISSING? Listen again, and complete the jokes with the missing words or phrases.

_____ home very late _____ night, Adam _____ Eve _____ angrily. "Late _____," she _____. "You _____ be seeing _____ other woman."

"I _____ that _____ wildly _____," _____ the outraged Adam. "_____ know _____ well that you and _____ are _____ alone in _____ world."

With _____, Adam _____ for the night. But _____ soon _____ him to _____ with a _____. There, _____ over _____, was Eve _____ counting his _____.

75

Morris was _____ at _____ by his _____,

_____ _____ _____, "If I were to die, _____ _____ _____ married again?"

"_____ a _____ at this time ____ ____ _____," he mumbled.

"Would ____ ____ _____ again?" she _____.

"Yeah," he admitted. "I _____ ____. _____."

"Would you _____ _____ to live here in _____ _____?"

"This is a ridiculous _____," he _____ drowsily, "but ____ ____ _____ _____, so why shouldn't we live here?"

"Would ____ _____ _____ ____ _____?"

The husband _____. "Why not? It's a _____, and it's less _____ a ____ _____. Yeah, _____ give her your _____."

"What about ____ _____ _____?"

"No," _____ replied _____. "I _____ give her _____ _____ _____."

"Why not?"

"_____," he said, " _____ _____."

Follow It Up

Apply your new knowledge and use your new vocabulary by doing the exercises that follow.

1. WORKING TOGETHER. In pairs, write a dialog or short story using at least ten words or expressions that appear in Part II of this unit. (It doesn't have to be funny.)

_____

_____

_____

_____

_____

2. FINDING SYNONYMS. Write a word or expression from this unit that is similar in meaning to the underlined words.

1. How much support money do you pay your ex-wife each week? _____

   _____

2. Do you have an agreement you signed with your fiancée before you

   got married? _____

3. Did you experience deep sadness after your teacher died? _____

4. Have you ever met anybody who had been removed by force from his

   or her home? _____

5. What is the most common disease in your country? _____

3. COMPLETING SENTENCES. Fill in the blanks with words from this list. Be sure to use the correct form.

extramarital affair	accusation	pout	cynic
calculating	hovering	rib	decent
painstakingly	image	lousy	absurd

1. The fine _____ I had of you was destroyed when I heard you

   cheated in the game.

2. Julie _____ and cried, but it didn't do any good. Her parents

   left her at home with the babysitter.

3. Most people are not surprised when businesspeople seem very

   _____.

4. Making me wait for two hours was a _____ thing to do.

5. I think I broke one of my _____ when I fell off my bicycle.

6. Mark is a _____ person. He would never hurt anybody on

   purpose.

7. After Jack had an _____, his wife left him.

8. It's easy to become a _____ when you see so many marriages

   failing.

9. Please stop _____ over me. It makes me nervous when you

   stand so close.

10. Your _____ is _____! How could you think I would steal from my own sister?

11. The surgeon _____ operated for six hours and saved the man's life.

Take It Further

1. Recreate one of the jokes you heard in this unit in your own words. Tell it for laughs if you wish.
2. Tell us about marriage in your country:
    a. How do people find their marriage partners? (Are matchmakers employed to find marriage partners?)
    b. Are most marriages based on love or on convenience?
    c. What is expected of the husband and wife? What roles are they expected to assume, and what are their responsibilities? Are they regarded as equal partners? Have their roles changed over the years, and if so, why and how?
    d. Is there a double standard regarding marital fidelity? How is cheating regarded?
    e. Is divorce an acceptable practice? Is it common? What are typical grounds for divorce? How are divorced people regarded in your country?
3. Why do you think so many marriages in America end in divorce? Is there a solution to this problem?
4. Do you think that jokes about marriage, cheating, and divorce are appropriate? Explain.
5. Read these short jokes carefully. Then discuss what they tell us about traditional American views of love, marriage, and divorce.
    a. Myron Cohen (a comedian):

    > Marriage is the only cure for love. All these fifty years I've been married, I have never thought about divorce. Murder, yes.

    b. Zsa Zsa Gabor (an actress):

    > A man in love is not complete until he is married. Then he is finished.

    c. Joan Rivers (a comedian):

    > Trust your husband, adore your husband, and get as much as you can in your name.

6. Now compare the views in the three jokes above, as you understand them, with those in your society.

Ethnic Humor

PART I

"Well, there goes the neighborhood!"

Get Ready

Do the GET READY activities before listening to the comedian's jokes and commentary. These activities will help you understand the comedian.

1. LET'S TALK. Ethnic jokes, which are based on stereotypes, can be dangerous and harmful, yet they are frequently told. Why do you think this is so? How do you feel about ethnic jokes? Do you tell them yourself? If so, about whom?

2. BUILD YOUR VOCABULARY. Try to guess the meanings of the words in bold italics.

1. Of course the drawing doesn't look exactly like me! The artist did a *caricature*, exaggerating all of my worst features.
2. Don't call me a *dum-dum* just because I don't know how to drive a car. I'm smart enough to learn, but I'm not interested.
3. The police officer didn't die when the thief shot him, because he was wearing his *bulletproof vest*.
4. America is described as a *melting pot*, because people who came from many different countries live together and adopt many of the customs that are considered "American."
5. Please write your name in the *blank* space provided at the top of your paper.
6. No matter how angry you are, don't be *abusive*. It won't help you if you hurt someone else.
7. While your math teacher is out sick, I will take his place and be your *substitute*.
8. The heart and the brain are two of the many *organs* of the body that you can't live without.
9. Steve was so *conceited* that he thought nobody could ever beat him in a race.
10. You're a *hypocrite*, because you tell people not to smoke and yet you still do.

Here are some additional words you will need to know. Check the Glossary for any of these words you don't understand.

apologized	immigrant	overseas	stereo
artificial	initially	peanut butter sandwich	villa
Danish	linen paper	remiss	
explorer	minorities	Riviera	

☺☺ 3. PREVIEW THESE SENTENCES. Listen to the Preview Sentences for Unit Six, Part I. Then fill in the missing words. You may check your answers on page 142.

1. This belief can be found even in the United States, which has always

   opened its doors to _____ and is considered the largest

   _____ in the world.

2. Try to remember that these jokes are only _____ of the
   _____; no race, creed, or color has the corner on
   _____, and any joke about one group of people can be
   easily applied to another.

3. The _____ is to protect yourself from being hurt; you'll
   need your imagination and sense of humor for obvious reasons, and
   your pen to fill in the _____ spaces that would normally
   contain the name of an ethnic group but which we have omitted in
   cases where the joke might be considered _____.

4. Did you hear about the "blank" scientist who developed an
   _____ appendix?

5. We can be real _____, complaining about problems we
   ourselves created.

**Make sure you understand what the sentences mean before you
continue.**

Now, Let's Laugh

☻☻ Listen to the comedian. Then decide if the statements you hear at
the end of the monologue are true or false. You may check your
answers on page 159.

Write your answers here.

1. Christopher Columbus landed in Spain in 1492. _____

2. The names of some ethnic groups have been omitted from these jokes.

   _____

3. An artificial appendix is a useful organ. _____

4. Americans rarely buy international products. _____

5. All women react romantically to their husbands' kisses. _____

Check Yourself

◎ ◎ Listen to the comedian again before you do the exercises. When you have finished, check your answers on pages 159–160 and 143.

1. COMPREHENSION CHECK. Answer each question with a sentence.

1. How do some people react when they hear others criticized or made fun of? _____

2. Why is it funny that the man who had a peanut butter sandwich for lunch every day threw it out? _____
_____

3. In the joke about the "typical American," why is he considered a hypocrite? _____
_____

4. When three men were told they could have anything they wanted because they had only six months to live, what did each want, and who was the most practical? _____
_____
_____

2. WHAT'S MISSING? Listen again, and complete the jokes.

The _____ man went home _____ complained _____ his _____. "I _____ Howard _____ downtown _____ morning and he _____ even _____ to me. I _____ he thinks I'm not his equal."

His wife _____, "Why, _____ stupid, _____, conceited, _____ Howard Smith. You _____ are his _____!"

How _____ the _____ American who _____ home from _____ French _____ in _____ German car, sits _____ Danish _____ in _____ Italian

_____, drinks _____ coffee _____ of _____ china, _____ to a _____ stereo, and _____ a _____ on _____ linen paper _____ to his _____ that _____ many American _____ are going _____?

Follow It Up

Apply your new knowledge and vocabulary in the exercises that follow.

1. WORKING TOGETHER. Write questions using five to ten words or expressions that appear in this part of Unit Six. Then ask your partner the questions.

_____

_____

_____

_____

_____

_____

_____

_____

_____

_____

_____

2. FINDING SYNONYMS. Write a word or expression from this unit that is similar in meaning to the underlined words.

1. Forgive me for being so <u>careless</u>. I know I should have called you, but I forgot. _____

2. I wrote my name in the <u>empty</u> space. Is that all right? _____

3. Do you agree with that <u>exaggerated description</u> of a college student?

   _____

4. I told you I was sorry many times. _____

5. Many <u>people living in Denmark</u> speak several languages. _____

3. COMPLETING SENTENCES. Fill in the blanks with words from the list. Then write a short answer to each question.

bulletproof vest	Riviera	abusive	remiss
Irish linen	explorer	artificial	initially
melting pot	overseas	hypocrite	immigrant

1. Do you know which _____ discovered your country? _____

   _____

2. What is it like to be an _____ in a strange new country?

   _____

3. Did you ever wear a _____ just like a police officer or

   a detective? _____

4. Do you ever use _____ language to your parents? _____

   _____

5. Have you ever been to the French _____? _____

   _____

6. How many times have you traveled _____? _____

   _____

7. Are you ever _____ about writing to your relatives? _____

   _____

8. Do you think America is truly a _____? _____

   _____

9. Have you ever written on really good paper, like _____?

   _____

10. Do you think people are _____ if they complain about

    their country's economy and then buy imported goods? _____

    _____

11. Now you seem to like speaking English, but _____, didn't you

    find it hard? _____

12. I know I shouldn't ask, but I will. Are your diamonds real or

    _____? _____

PART II

"Does that mean I have to eat cornflakes?"

Get Ready

1. BUILD YOUR VOCABULARY. Try to guess the meanings of the words in bold italics.

1. Our teachers' **union** voted to stop working until we get a better salary offer, so I won't be teaching today. Sorry!
2. When I said I need your money like I need a second head, I was being **facetious**. Actually, I really do need a loan.
3. Sometime, somebody will **expose** your activities. Everybody should know that you're working for a criminal.
4. Donald Magnum is a **traitor**. We thought he was our friend, but in fact, he's our enemy.
5. Even though religious leaders—men and women **of the cloth**—are always expected to do the right thing, they have the right to make mistakes, too.
6. You couldn't be perfect; surely, you have one or two **vices**, like smoking or drinking.
7. I have **confessed** all of my sins. Now it's your turn to tell me what you have done wrong.
8. Living in a rural area doesn't make me a **hillbilly**. I read the newspapers, and I know what's going on in this world.

9. After Kathleen Turner made her second big movie, she was a **sensation**. Everybody started talking about how great she was.
10. Walking **backwards**, instead of forward, is not natural behavior.
11. How about **barbecuing** that steak outdoors rather than cooking it in the house?
12. We don't have a bathroom in the house. You'll have to use the **outhouse**.
13. Next time you have to take the train, tell me. I'll be glad to drive you to the **depot**.
14. I am **contemplating** leaving this town. I haven't decided yet, but I'm giving it a lot of thought.

Here are some additional words you will need to know. Check the Glossary for any of these words you don't understand.

authentic	dweller	native	rural
backyard	gossip	Navajo Indian	scotch
Baptist	grill	pickup truck	threaten
border	Hollywood	pork	transgression
confidential	lifestyle	priest	
Dutch	Methodist minister	rabbi	

⊕⊕ **2. PREVIEW THESE SENTENCES.** Listen to the Preview Sentences for Unit Six, Part II. Then fill in the missing words. You may check your answers on page 144.

1. He _____ to _____ the _____ and have him thrown out of their professional organization.

2. Four men _____ were having a _____ talk discussing their _____.

3. Well, how about the _____ singer who went to _____ and became a _____?

4. As a country boy, he probably wasn't familiar with the tradition of _____ food on a _____ outside, and he wasn't used to having the bathroom in the house.

5. Whether we arrived in the United States yesterday or several years ago, or are still _____ our trip, we're all subject to jokes.

Make sure you understand what the sentences mean before you continue.

86

Now, Let's Laugh

😊😊 Listen to the comedian. Then decide if the statements you hear at the end of the monologue are true or false. You may check your answers on page 160.

Write your answers here.

1. Rembrandt is a famous housepainter. _____

2. According to the joke, various religious leaders have vices. _____

3. If you're a stranger in the city, you shouldn't take everything you see and hear literally. _____

4. The best way to catch a rabbit is to put salt on its tail. _____

5. The authentic hosts of America are hillbillies. _____

Check Yourself

😊😊 Listen to the comedian again before you do the exercises. When you have finished, check your answers on pages 160 and 144.

1. COMPREHENSION CHECK. Answer each question with a sentence.

1. How did Fred, the housepainter, respond to the homeowner, Mr. Brown, who said he wouldn't pay Rembrandt that kind of money? Why was Fred's response funny? _____

_____

2. To what vice did the Methodist minister admit? _____

_____

3. What was wrong with the way the person in the pick-up truck responded to the traffic signals? _____

_____

4. Why did the hillbilly think they did everything backwards in California? _____

5. What did the Navajo Indian mean when he said, "How do you like our country?" What is ironic about the Indians' position in America? _____

_____

_____

2. WHAT'S MISSING? Listen again, and complete the jokes.

The _____, Mr. Brown, asked _____ "blank"

_____, Fred, _____ he would _____ to

_____ his _____.

"_____ dollars _____ day _____ man—

_____ the _____," _____ answered.

"You've _____ _____ be _____," Brown said.   "I

_____ pay _____ that _____ of _____."

"I _____ news for _____," said the "blank"

housepainter.   "_____ that _____ charges _____

_____ less, _____ throw him _____ of the

_____."

_____ men _____ _____ _____ were _____ a

_____ talk _____ their _____.

"_____ like _____," the rabbi _____.   "I

_____ a _____ of _____ a day," said the

_____.   "I _____ a girlfriend,"

_____ the _____.   They _____ turned to the

_____ minister, who _____.   "Me? I _____ to

_____."

Follow It Up

Apply your new knowledge and vocabulary in the exercises that follow.

1. WORKING TOGETHER.   In pairs, write a dialog or short story using at least ten words or expressions from Part II of this unit.

_____

_____

_____

_____

_____

2. FINDING SYNONYMS. Write a word or expression from this unit that is similar in meaning to the underlined words.

1. Did you <u>admit</u> your sins to the priest? _____

2. I live in a <u>countrylike</u> area. _____

3. The <u>leader of the Jewish synagogue</u> was talking to a group of children.

_____

4. He <u>warned</u> me before I went to the police. _____

5. This memo is <u>top-secret</u>. _____

6. It's a bad idea to <u>tell stories</u> about your friends and their private lives.

_____

7. I'll meet you at the <u>railroad station</u>. _____

8. Our <u>workers' organization</u> is very strong. _____

9. Pieter isn't German; he's <u>from Holland</u>. _____

10. Are you <u>thinking about</u> moving? _____

3. COMPLETING SENTENCES. Fill in the blanks with words from this list.

native	transgression	sensation	vice
dweller	barbecuing	lifestyle	scotch
traitor	authentic	outhouse	pork

1. If you are a city _____, you may not like life in the country.

2. He created a _____ when he sang his most popular songs.

3. You'll get very sick if you drink too much _____.

4. I'll be a _____ if I tell you Janet's secret.

5. Most people from the city are not used to using an _____.

6. Since I was born here, I consider myself a _____ American.

7. I don't know if this will is _____. It looks as though
somebody changed it.

8. Since I've made many mistakes in my life, I can forgive your

_____.

9. Are you _____ those hamburgers and hot dogs on a grill?

10. Certain groups of people are not supposed to eat _____.

11. After our children were born, our _____ changed considerably.
We rarely had time to travel.

12. I can't believe you have no _____. Nobody is perfect.

Take It Further

1. In your own words, recreate one of the jokes you heard in this unit. Either summarize the events of the joke, or try to tell it for laughs.
2. Have you ever been the butt of an ethnic joke? Explain what happened and how you reacted.
3. How do you react when you hear ethnic jokes?
4. Are ethnic jokes popular in your country? What groups of people are often the butt of humor? Why?
5. What groups of people have you heard jokes about in America?
6. Is your country a melting pot, or are the people homogeneous? What are the advantages and disadvantages of living in either a heterogeneous or a homogeneous society? (This may be discussed, initially, in small groups.)
7. What have you heard about the American Indian? Do you have a similar group of people who are the authentic natives in your country? What is their situation today? How have they been treated?
8. Do you have unions in your country? Why or why not? Are they powerful? What have you heard about American unions? Do you approve of unions? What are the advantages and disadvantages of belonging to a union? (This may be discussed, initially, in small groups.)
9. What are the most prevalent religions in your country? How do they differ? Do they coexist peacefully?
10. Read the following jokes, and explain why they are funny.

    a. There was a "blank" soldier whose sergeant told him to stand at the end of the line. The "blank" soldier came back and said, "There's somebody there already."

    b. Two "blanks" met on Fifth Avenue, and one yelled, "Say, Frank, I haven't seen you for years. Golly, you've changed. You used to be fat, now you're thin. You used to have hair, now you're bald. You never had a beard, now you have a beard. You were tall, but now you seem shorter—golly, how you've changed, Frank."

    The other "blank" says, "My name isn't Frank."

    And the first "blank" replies, "Oh, you've changed your *name*, too?"

    c. The doctor gave strict instructions to his "blank" patient: "No starches, no sweets, and you can only smoke one cigar a day." A week later the "blank" returned looking worse than ever. His face was almost green. "What happened?" the doctor asked.

    "You and your lousy instructions!" the "blank" cried. "I cut out the starches and sweets, but that one cigar a day darn near killed me. I never smoked before in my life."

    d. Once upon a time, there were two "blank" astronauts. They were circling the globe in outer space. One of the astronauts was sent to walk outside the capsule to see what was happening. A half hour later he was back, and he knocked on the door of the space ship. The astronaut inside asked, "Who's there?"

"Sunny California"

"The view is even better at this level!"

Get Ready

Do the GET READY activities before listening to the comedian's jokes and commentary. These activities will help you understand the comedian.

1. LET'S TALK. One of America's best humorists is Art Buchwald. For many years, he has been writing humorous columns that appear in daily newspapers. More than 200 of these columns have been collected in his Pulitzer-prizewinning book, *Laid Back in Washington*. In this unit, you will hear one of his columns about Los Angeles, California.

Most people, no matter where they live, have heard about California, USA. Many people, even Americans who live in other states, dream about visiting the romantic state where movies are made, life appears to be casual, and the scenery is breathtaking. How do *you* visualize life in California? What have you heard, read in books, or seen in person, on television, or in the movies? Share your thoughts and experiences before you listen to Mr. Art Buchwald's unusual conversation with his California friends in Los Angeles.

2. BUILD YOUR VOCABULARY. Try to guess the meanings of the words in bold italics.

1. When Jill isn't working, she likes to read, paint, dance, and play tennis for *recreation*.
2. I'm *bailing out* the water in the boat so that it won't sink.
3. Many trees on the mountain were destroyed by a *mud slide*. Half the mountain slid down to the shore.
4. The flat land of the *plains* is a good place for you to build your home.
5. The *brushfire* is spreading so quickly that all the houses on the side of the hill are in danger of being destroyed.
6. It's kind of *hairy* to watch a fire burning in a house next to yours. You'd be scared, too.
7. The water in the streams and rivers is overflowing as a result of the *deluge* we had yesterday.
8. My mail has mistakenly been delivered to several of my neighbors recently. I wonder where my paycheck will *wind up* next.
9. Your family has moved four times in the last two years. Don't you think it's time for you to finally *settle down* and stay in one place?
10. We're never going to reduce the *smog* in this city if we continue to burn our trash as often as we do. It's hard to see across the street.

Here are some additional words you will need to know. Check the Glossary for any of these words you don't understand.

canyon	Jacuzzi	stuck
drought	patio	
earthquake	rain forest	

☺☺ **3. PREVIEW THESE SENTENCES.** Listen to the Preview Sentences for Unit Seven. Then fill in the missing words. You may check your answers on page 146.

1. I came to Los Angeles last week for rest and _____, only to

   discover that it had become a _____.

2. "Why do you build your house on the top of a _____ when you

   know that during a rainstorm it has a good chance of sliding away?"

3. "Still, it must be kind of _____ to sit in your home during a

   _____ and wonder where you'll _____ next."

4. "Sure we have floods, and fire and _____, but that's the price

   you pay for living the good life."

5. "We would wake up in the morning and listen to the birds, and eat

   breakfast out on the _____ and look down on the

   _____."

Make sure you understand what the sentences mean before you
continue.

Now, Let's Laugh

😊😊 Listen to the comedian. Then decide if the statements you hear at
the end of the monologue are true or false. You may check your
answers on page 160.

Write your answers here.

1. The author went to Los Angeles on business. _____

2. The Cables own a mobile home. _____

3. The Cables bought the house because of the neighbors. _____

4. Sunny California never has floods. _____

5. If the Cables' house slides too far, they'll consider moving. _____

Check Yourself

😊😊 Listen to the comedian again before you do the exercises. When
you have finished, check your answers on pages 160 and 147.

1. COMPREHENSION CHECK. Answer each question
with a sentence.

1. Why had the Cables' house moved a few times? _____

   _____

2. The Cables didn't seem to care that their house slid. How did they

   see themselves benefitting from this situation? _____

   _____

3. Do houses seem to be expensive or inexpensive in Los Angeles? How can you tell? _____

_____

4. What types of problems do people living in this area have to deal with?

_____

5. What will the Cables do if their house slides too far? _____

_____

2. WHAT'S MISSING? Listen again, and complete these paragraphs.

"_____ hard _____ people who _____ live

_____ California _____ understand _____ we people

_____ out _____. Sure _____ have floods,

_____ fire and _____, but _____ the _____

you _____ to pay _____ living the _____ _____. When

Esther and _____ saw _____ house, we _____ it

_____ a _____ come _____. It was _____

right _____ the _____ top _____ the _____

way _____ there. We _____ wake _____ in the

_____ and _____ ___ the birds, and _____ breakfast

_____ on _____ patio and _____ down

_____ the _____.

"Then _____ the _____ mud slide, we found

_____ living next to _____. It was _____ entirely

different _____. _____ by that _____ we were

ready for a _____. _____ we've _____ again, and

_____ in a _____ new _____. You

_____ do that if you live _____ solid _____.

_____ you move _____ a house _____ Sunset

Boulevard, _____ stuck _____ for the _____ of your

life. When you _____ on the _____ of a hill in _____

_____, you _____ least know _____ not _____

to _____ forever."

94

Follow It Up

Apply your new knowledge and vocabulary in the exercises that follow.

1. WORKING TOGETHER. In pairs, write a dialog or short story using at least ten words or expressions from this unit. (It doesn't have to be funny.)

_____

_____

_____

_____

_____

_____

_____

2. FINDING SYNONYMS. Answer each question with a sentence that uses a synonym from this unit for the underlined words.

1. Doesn't the fog and smoke in the air bother you? _____

   _____

2. What do you like to do for fun and rest? _____

   _____

3. Have you ever been in an area affected by no rain? _____

   _____

4. When do you plan to stay in one place for a long time? _____

   _____

5. Do you know where you'll finally be after you finish your education?

   _____

3. COMPLETING SENTENCES. Fill in the blanks with words from this list.

earthquake	plains	patio	rainstorm
bailing out	Jacuzzi	hairy	

1. Would you rather live in the hills or on the _____?

2. Many homes and buildings were destroyed during the

   _____.

3. People enjoy relaxing in a _____.

4. Do you think an umbrella will help you if you are walking in a

   _____?

5. Flying in an airplane that's having engine trouble is a _____

   experience.

6. I'm _____ my car because the windows were down when it

   rained last night.

7. It's such a lovely night for sitting outside on the _____.

Take It Further

1. What do the Cables consider the good life?
2. Mr. Buchwald describes the good life in California ironically. Discuss how he does this.
3. What kind of people do you think the Cables are? Do you think they have a healthy attitude? How did you arrive at this conclusion? What do you know about them and their way of thinking?
4. California is known to have problems with nature. Particular areas are threatened with earthquakes, and others are often badly affected by brushfires, drought, mud slides, and smog. Also, it's very expensive to live in California. Why do you think people still choose to live there?
5. What do you consider "the good life"? With a partner, create a situation that you consider ideal for living. (This might include a particular profession, location, economic status, family and friends, position in society or the community, possessions, etc.)
6. Do you prefer to live in a busy, crowded city where there is a lot of activity, or do you prefer to live in a quiet area in the country, in the mountains, or near the seashore? Explain.
7. Explain what is funny about the following jokes:

   a. I came here during the smog, felt the sights, and went home.

   b. There are more cars here in California than in Italy, Germany, and Belgium put together. There is only one solution: we'll have to park overseas.

   c. Everything in California is drive-ins: drive-in theaters, drive-in churches, drive-in restaurants, and so on. The only time you get out of your car is to make a trade.

   d. California is great: on a clear day—when the fog lifts—you can see the smog.

8. Ask someone (except, perhaps, a Californian) to explain this joke.

   QUESTION: How many Californians does it take to wash a car?

   ANSWER: Four. One to do the washing and three to share the experience.

Health, Diet, and Exercise

"And how many sit-ups do I have to do for a piece of pizza?"

Get Ready

Do the GET READY activities before listening to the comedian's jokes and commentary. These activities will help you understand the comedian.

1. LET'S TALK. Who are the "beautiful" people in America? If you look in a popular American magazine, or turn on the TV, you are certain to see very slender, physically fit people involved in some form of activity. Gone are the days when *plump* was considered pleasant and exercise was the pastime of the athlete or the chronologically young.

Now, few people are permitted to get old peacefully. What has happened to change America's model American? Why is there such a *preoccupation* with thinness and exercise? Share your thoughts before you find out what Americans are doing to stay in shape.

2. BUILD YOUR VOCABULARY. Try to guess the meanings of the words in bold italics.

1. I didn't plan to accept Jack's marriage proposal, but I couldn't help it. I **succumbed** when he promised to support me through law school.
2. Now that I am **trimmer**, I can fit into a smaller pair of pants than I could last year.
3. You're not supposed to eat candy, pizza, or cake in your diet. Your **conscience** will bother you if you do.
4. I eat very little, yet I find it difficult to stay thin. I'm losing the **battle of the bulge**.
5. The arguments at the office are giving me a lot of **aggravation**. They really upset me.
6. The telephone company will send me a **disconnect notice**, and I will lose the use of my phone, if I don't pay their bill by the end of this week.
7. Every week Jeff has a new **flame**. I wonder which girl he's in love with this week.
8. I am firing you because you **plagiarized**. How could you copy my report and sign your name?
9. I believe there has been a mistake; I wasn't **credited** for working this weekend.
10. As soon as I saw Nancy **collapsing** from the heat, I ran over and tried to stop her from falling.
11. All the unkind things Max did were **obliterated** when he saved a little boy's life. We forgot all his bad deeds.
12. You're going to fall down from **exhaustion** if you don't get more rest.
13. The milk and eggs will spoil if you don't close the **fridge** tightly.
14. I'd love to go to a **resort** for a few days. I need a place where I can play tennis, swim, and relax.
15. You **betrayed** me. I thought I could trust you, but I was wrong.
16. There is no way you can **circumvent** the truth. None of your stories will prevent us from finding out what really happened.
17. Don't **make light of** dieting when you are with Emily. She takes this subject very seriously.
18. I've heard Richie describe how the accident occurred. What's your **version**?
19. You **stunned** me when you said you were getting a divorce. I was really shocked.
20. "Two" and "to" are **homonyms**. They have the same sound but different meanings.

Here are some additional words you will need to know. Check
the Glossary for any of these words you don't understand.

aerobic dancing	glazed doughnut	muscles	spa
Beverly Hills	hot fudge sundae	network	stroke (n.)
calories	jogging	outdoorsman	swallow (v.)
chopstick	limburger cheese	plague (v.)	sweat (v.)
colleague	liniment	plump	tranquilizer
frankfurter	Madison Avenue	preoccupation	utensils
garlic	mortal	snack	vodka

⊙⊙ **3. PREVIEW THESE SENTENCES.** Listen to the
Preview Sentences for Unit Eight. Then fill in the missing words. You
may check your answers on page 147.

1. After a lifetime of eating the foods I enjoy, and using my _____
   as little as possible, I have _____ to
   _____ image of the fit and attractive American,
   and I've changed my lifestyle.

2. My hands are faster. I can get more in my mouth before my
   _____ takes over.

3. Open mail and find final _____ from telephone
   company, a threatening letter from spouse of new _____, and
   a note from a friend informing you that you have been recently
   _____ on _____ television.

4. People today are running, jumping, _____, and
   _____.

5. Of course, the exercise they get walking from the TV to the refrigerator
   is _____ by the fattening _____ they get from the
   _____.

6. They can't believe that with all they've done through proper diet and
   exercise to _____ the laws of nature, they are,
   nevertheless, _____ and will eventually die.

**Make sure you understand what the sentences mean before you
continue.**

Now, Let's Laugh

◎ ◎   Listen to the comedian. Then decide if the statements you hear in the middle of the monologue are true or false. You may check your answers on page 160.

Write your answers here.

1. On the Harry Secombe diet, you drink vodka all day. _____

2. Cigarettes have a lot of calories. _____

3. On the Fran Leibowitz diet, you can eat fattening foods. _____

4. You can lose a lot of weight on the tranquilizer diet. _____

5. Many people are more concerned about counting calories than the cost of their meals. _____

Check Yourself

◎ ◎   Listen to the comedian again before you do the exercises. When you have finished, check your answers on pages 160–161, 149, and 150.

1. COMPREHENSION CHECK.   Answer each question with a sentence.

1. What two kinds of books sell best in any bookstore? What is interesting about their relationship to each other? _____

2. Describe one of the diets mentioned on the tape, and explain its flaw (that is, tell what's wrong with it). _____

3. Why doesn't the speaker like Fran Leibowitz's diet? _____

4. Give an example that shows how preoccupied Americans are with counting calories. _____

5. Why is jogging considered good for the economy? _____

6. Why is getting sick a problem for people who watch their diets and exercise frequently? _____

7. Does the speaker appear to be happy about dieting and exercise? What words, expressions, and thoughts helped express the speaker's feelings on this subject?_____

_____

_____

2. WHAT'S MISSING? Listen again, and complete the paragraphs.

Frankly, I _____ gladly _____ without _____

doughnuts _____ I _____ _____ those problems.

_____ the _____ of _____ _____ is _____

_____ in _____ _____. But _____ to be _____

by the _____ ____ ____ man I just _____ _____ would

_____ about _____ me running. My _____ is more

_____ than _____ and _____. And then

_____ find _____ that the _____ I _____ _____

_____ years _____ was now being _____ on

television _____ my _____ _____ for it would just about

_____ _____ over the _____. I think _____ the

_____ of _____ on this _____ of _____, I

would _____ _____ a stroke. No, I _____ think _____

_____ it. _____ be _____ off _____ those

_____. But _____ you _____, _____

Leibowitz, for the _____.

Well, _____ _____ don't _____ _____ _____ seriously,

____ _____ they _____ different _____ of exercise.

Joey Adams _____ his _____ _____ of exercise is _____

shop _____. I _____ see ____ _____. Just

_____ of all _____ _____ from one _____ to

_____. The _____ she _____, the more

_____ she burns. _____ makes _____.

Follow It Up

Apply your new knowledge and vocabulary in the exercises that follow.

1. WORKING TOGETHER. In pairs, describe some of the diets you've heard about, and explain what's wrong with them. *Or* create your own questions about the passage you just heard, and then ask your partner your questions. Use as many of the words and expressions from the unit as you can.

_____

_____

_____

_____

_____

_____

_____

_____

2. FINDING SYNONYMS. Write words or expressions from this unit that are similar in meaning to the underlined words.

1. He <u>copied</u> my article and sold it to a magazine. _____

2. Don't try to <u>go around</u> the problem. _____

3. Have you met Mary Wilson, a <u>person I work with</u>? _____

4. After working ten hours straight, I'm ready to drop from <u>fatigue</u>. _____

_____

5. I need a <u>medicine that can calm my nerves</u>. _____

6. This cold <u>bothers</u> me day and night. _____

7. You certainly are looking <u>slimmer</u>! _____

8. Michael doesn't like to believe that he is just like the rest of us,

   <u>capable of dying</u>. _____

9. This is serious business. Please don't <u>joke about</u> my problem. _____

_____

10. My problem is <u>staying thin</u>. _____

3. COMPLETING SENTENCES. Fill in the blanks with words from this list.

conscience	snack	stunned	resort
fridge	flame	network	garlic
credit	liniment	aerobic dancing	version
utensil	preoccupation	glazed doughnut	

1. Did you put the milk and eggs in the _____?

2. Is that young woman your new _____?

3. Don't have a steak sandwich at 4:00. A _____ is supposed to be small and light.

4. Why didn't you call your boss when you stayed home from work? I _____ you with having more common sense.

5. I usually have two _____ with my morning coffee.

6. You'd better rub _____ on your sore muscles.

7. I don't care how you eat at home, but here we eat with _____. Use your fork.

8. Danny _____ us all when he lost twenty pounds. We were so surprised.

9. I called the television _____ to complain when they took off my favorite show.

10. I must tell you the truth because my _____ is bothering me.

11. This sauce is very tasty. How much _____ did you put in it?

12. Which _____ are you staying at in Hawaii?

13. He has a great _____ with jazz. He won't even listen to other kinds of music.

14. I don't like running, but _____ is fun. I can do just about anything to music.

15. My _____ of the events leading to Amy and Tom's divorce is different from yours. I guess we see things very differently.

Take It Further

1. Recreate one of the jokes you heard in this unit in your own words.
2. In your country:
   a. Who are "the beautiful people"? What do they look like? What characteristics do they have in common? Has the image of "beautiful" people changed? If so, in what way, and why has this change occurred?
   b. Is yours a youth-oriented and physically fit society? Are health clubs and cosmetic, or plastic, surgeons doing much business in your country?
   c. How is old age regarded in your country? Do people fear it? Are the elderly treated as wise and useful or as the opposite?
   d. About what kinds of health problems do people in your country seem to be concerned? What is being done about these problems?
2. What is your description of a "beautiful person"?
3. Do you like to eat or do something that you know isn't good for your health? Make a list of and share your "bad" habits.
4. Describe your diet. Is it a special kind?
5. What would you prescribe for people who want to live longer?
6. For fun, pretend you are employees in an advertising agency that produces commercials for television, radio, newspapers, or magazines. In pairs, choose a particular medium (TV, radio, newspaper, or magazine) and a particular product (for example, vitamins, a diet cookbook, an exercise machine, a health club, diet pills, or cosmetic surgery). Then create an advertisement that would appeal to America's preoccupation with good health, youth, and physical attractiveness. Your commercial could be a dialog, a poster, a cartoon, or whatever you wish. Let your imagination be your guide.
7. Explain the following jokes:

   a. Diets are strictly for those who are thick and tired of it.

   b. The second day of a diet is always easier than the first. By the second day, you're off it.

   c. Sign in reducing salon: "Rear today—gone tomorrow."

   d. "No rich foods, no meat, no drinks," the doctor prescribed to his patient. "That should save you enough money to pay my bills."

   e. If you are thin, don't eat fast.
      If you are fat, don't eat. Fast.

   f. The travels of a French fried potato: in your mouth a second, in your stomach four hours, on your hips the rest of your life.

   g. "I get plenty of exercise," says comedian *Jackie Gleason*. "Immediately after waking, I always say sternly to myself, 'Ready now. Up. Down. Up. Down. And after three strenuous minutes, I tell myself, 'Okay, boy. Now we'll try the other eyelid.'"

   h. There are so many exciting miracle drugs around, I'm sorry I'm healthy. I'm missing all the fun.

Travel, American Style

"Thank goodness we're home. Now I'll take a vacation."

Get Ready

Do the GET READY activities before listening to the comedian's jokes and commentary. These activities will help you understand the comedian.

1. LET'S TALK. Many Americans count the days until their next vacation. And as they are returning home from one trip, the chances are they are discussing plans for their next one. Of course, not everybody will agree on what *constitutes* a vacation. Some people enjoy sleeping in the "great outdoors," while others demand the luxuries of a comfortable hotel. Before you explore the *trials and tribulations* of our American vacationers, discuss your own dream vacations. What is your ideal vacation?

2. BUILD YOUR VOCABULARY. Try to guess the meanings of the words in bold italics.

1. It seems *everybody and his brother* is driving on this road. Why is it so crowded?
2. You appear to be *artistically* inclined. All of your photographs are unusual and creative.
3. Edie is quite *sophisticated*. She seems to know a lot about life.
4. Jane couldn't handle her job. She was *overwhelmed* by all of the work she had to do.
5. We were supposed to land in Spain, but two men with guns *hijacked* our plane and forced us to land in France.
6. I'm sorry about calling you so late. I didn't think about the time. I just dialed *automatically*.
7. You can *activate* your machine by pressing the "on" button.
8. Can I use any of my United States *currency* to buy things in Canada and Mexico?
9. Your *liaisons* are well known in this city. The local newspapers have written about your love affairs several times this year.
10. I don't agree with your *tactics*. You can't stop me from taking another job by telling other companies I am not available.
11. My son lost an important soccer game. Excuse me while I try to *console* him. I hope I can make him feel better.
12. I hope you are rich this month. According to your *charge slips*, you owe the stores a lot of money.
13. My *morale* is very low. I've been depressed ever since I lost my job.
14. When we landed in Hawaii, our friends greeted us by saying, *"Aloha."* It seems to be their favorite expression.

Here are some additional words you will need to know. Check the Glossary for any of these words you don't understand.

abroad	destination	kennel	thoroughly
accommodations	franc	lawn	tips (n.)
burden	fret	lens	video
burglar alarm	ghastly	mow	
cruise	illusion	notify	
dangling	instamatic	terminal	

3. PREVIEW THESE SENTENCES. Listen to the Preview Sentences for Unit Nine. Then fill in the missing words. You may check your answers on pages 150–151.

1. For those who are _____ and _____ undemanding, there are inexpensive _____ that do just about everything automatically.

2. Usually, the only time a person looks that _____ is when his or her plane is being _____

3. There's transportation, food, _____, sightseeing tours, car rentals, _____, _____, and all sorts of other trivial things to consider.

4. Then we set the lights that go on _____, _____ the _____, and lock all the doors and windows.

5. He should have known I was referring to the French _____— the _____—not the American food—the _____.

6. But if you can't afford to go _____ this year, or on any vacation for that matter, don't _____; there are things you can do to give yourself and your friends the _____ of traveling.

Make sure you understand what the sentences mean before you continue.

Now, Let's Laugh

⊙⊙ Listen to the comedian. Now, surprise! You have new and different directions for your true-or-false questions. Listen even more carefully than usual to the tape, because you are going to make up five questions that you will ask your partner or the class.

Create statements that are either true or false, and write them here.

1. _____

2. _____

3. _____

4. _____

5. _____

Now let your classmates decide whether your statements are true or false.

Check Yourself

Listen to the comedian again before you do the exercises. When you have finished, check your answers on pages 161, 151, and 152.

1. COMPREHENSION CHECK. Answer each question with a sentence.

1. Based on what you heard, who are the people who board an airplane first? _____

_____

2. How can we identify a tourist? _____

3. What camera should the impatient photographer buy? _____

_____

4. Why do tourists take so many pictures? _____

5. What are some of the problems a traveler encounters? _____

_____

6. According to the joke, what is Alex's opinion of the travel book that is supposed to tell you how to have a wonderful vacation on $10 a day? What did he say to indicate this feeling? _____

_____

7. What impressed Mark Twain about the children of Paris? _____

_____

8. Why did the French have difficulty understanding Luke? What was wrong with his language education? _____

_____

9. Describe one way you can give yourself or your friends the illusion that you are on a vacation. _____

10. What is one advantage of staying home? _____

2. WHAT'S MISSING? Listen again, and complete the jokes.

Are _____ _____ necessary? _____, they _____,

_____ to _____ _____ _____ _____ taken a trip. Today,

the _____ is _____ _____ one _____ take __

_____; the _____ is, _____ _____? For _____ who

108

are _____ and _____ _____, there are

_____ instamatics that ____ _____ _____ everything

_____. Then _____ are _____ _____

with _____ kinds of _____ that _____ more

_____, _____, and work on the _____ of the

_____. And, __ course, we _____ the _____ movie

_____, which _____ people today ____ _____ in for _____

cameras that _____ in the _____ and _____ of _____

they _____.

_____ we _____ a _____, ____ the same _____.

We ____ ____ at ____ o'clock ____ the _____ to get an _____

_____. First we ____ _____; then ____ _____; then we

_____ the neighbors and _____ _____; then we _____ the

_____, _____, and _____ deliveries; then we _____

for a ____ to _____ the _____ and water ____ _____; then we

_____ the ____ to the _____; then the _____ say goodbye to _____

_____; then we set the _____ that ____ ____ automatically,

_____ the _____ _____, and lock all the _____ and

_____. _____ all this is _____ done, you _____ what

____ ____? We go ____ _____, because I _____ _____ _____!

Follow It Up

1. WORKING TOGETHER. In pairs, create a dialog using as many of the words or expressions from this unit as possible. Dialogs could involve two people discussing the pros and cons of taking a vacation or two people discussing their most recent vacation.

_____

_____

_____

_____

_____

_____

2. FINDING SYNONYMS. Answer each question with a sentence that uses a synonym from this unit for the underlined word or words.

1. Did you <u>start</u> the air-conditioning system? _____

   _____

2. How many <u>boat trips</u> to Europe have you taken? _____

   _____

3. What do you <u>worry</u> about? _____

4. What is that <u>hanging</u> from your neck? _____

5. Did you ever try to <u>comfort</u> someone when you were just as upset?

   _____

6. Was your <u>mood</u> low when you first arrived here? _____

   _____

3. COMPLETING SENTENCES. Fill in the blanks with words from this list.

lawn	lens	currency	everybody and his brother
hijacked	liaison	thoroughly	sophisticated
ghastly	tactics	overwhelmed	accommodations
kennel	video	terminal	

1. At ten o'clock in the morning, our plane was _____ and forced to land in Greece.

2. Did you mow the _____ yet?

3. You are very _____ for someone your age.

4. The _____ was very crowded this morning. I wasn't sure I would get a seat on the bus.

5. Don't leave a job half-done; do it _____.

6. We were _____ with joy when we saw our new baby.

7. Did you leave your dog in a _____ when you went on your trip?

8. I felt and looked _____ after my operation.

9. _____ watched that exciting World Series game.

10. Did you _____-tape the game so you could show it to your children?

11. The _____ in this hotel are great. We have such spacious rooms.

12. What _____ did you use to get the Mitchell Company to move to our city?

13. I'm sorry, but you don't have the right _____. You can't buy anything here with those coins.

14. William will make use of his various _____ when he gets to Washington and needs financial support.

15. Professional photographers use many different types of _____.

Take It Further

1. Recreate one of the jokes in this unit in your own words.
2. If you were planning a trip,
   a. where would you go?
   b. what would you take?
   c. what details would you take care of regarding accommodations, transportation, and the day of departure?
3. With a partner, work on a vacation itinerary for a ten-day or two-week vacation. Then tell the class, and state your reasons for your choice.
4. If an American were vacationing in your country, what places of interest should she or he visit? Are there special times of the year when certain places are more attractive?
5. What problems would a traveler encounter in your country? (Consider food, accommodations, transportation, utilities, shopping, safety, weather, etc.)
6. What souvenirs should one bring home from your country?
7. Share your travel experiences, especially the humorous ones. (Consider luggage inconveniences, transportation, weather, incompatible travel companions, etc.)
8. Explain the following jokes.

   a. When my wife packs for a trip, the only thing she leaves behind is a note for the milkman.

   b. After looking at a prospective tourist's passport photo, a fellow at a travel bureau commented, "If the owner really looks like that, he's too sick to travel."

c.   An American tourist who was gazing into the crater of a Greek volcano said, "It looks like Hell." "Oh, you Americans," said the guide, "you've been everywhere."

d.   The American tourists were being guided through an ancient castle in Italy. "This place is 500 years old," the guide said. "Not a stone in there has been touched, nothing fixed, nothing replaced, in all those years."

"Well," said one of the tourists from New York, "they must have the same landlord I've got."

e.   The tourist from Kansas City stopped at a small restaurant on the French Riviera. He ordered an ordinary ham sandwich, and the bill was six dollars. "Is ham so scarce?" the tourist asked the waiter in amazement.

"No, but American tourists are."

All Our Funny Friends

"Wait, that wasn't a joke!"

Get Ready

Do the GET READY activities before listening to the comedian's jokes and commentary. These activities will help you understand the comedian.

1. LET'S TALK. Now that you've been exposed to American humor in the previous units, are you more aware of the comedians we enjoy? Who are the funny Americans you've heard about or seen on television, in the movies, or on stage? Before we introduce you to many of our favorites, we ask you to "name names," and, if you can, tell what you think of them. Are they funny to you? Why or why not?

2. BUILD YOUR VOCABULARY. Try to guess the meanings of the words in bold italics.

1. I love everything about **show business**—the actors I work with, the costumes I put on, and even rehearsing my lines.
2. Tonight's dinner is a **fund-raising** event for our school. The money you pay for your dinner will be used to buy a new video camera for our theater department.
3. If you kill any of our people, we'll **retaliate** immediately. You can be sure we'll fight back.
4. We're going to offer free cookies to **promote** our new holiday cookie.
5. It is the **producer**'s job to get the money, actors, director, scenery, and costumes for the show.
6. After his **press agent** wrote a few articles about Jack's new play, many people came to the theater to see it.
7. I'm very **sentimental** about my childhood. I've saved my books, toys, and even items of clothing to remind me of the "good old days."
8. You sure are **gullible**. You seem to believe everything you hear even if it doesn't make sense.
9. I'd like to **unload** my car on somebody because it doesn't run well.
10. I think Jamie has really gone **off his rocker** and **lost all of his marbles**. He's downright crazy.
11. This shirt is so ugly *I wouldn't be found dead*—and certainly not alive—in it.
12. Sharon is so **handy** with the television equipment. She can fix anything that goes wrong with it.
13. I was so surprised when Arthur **modestly** said, "I couldn't have invented this machine without the help of my brother." He should have given himself more credit.
14. We didn't plan to go to the dance; we just **drifted in** after dinner.
15. You were just like a **life preserver**. You saved my life.
16. The students in my last class were not very **responsive**. They didn't answer my questions or seem interested in the subject.
17. The police were lucky. They **defused** the bomb one minute before it was going to explode.
18. What television shows do they make at this **studio**?
19. Giving food and clothing to poor families is a **worthy cause**.

Here are some additional words that you will need to know. Check the Glossary for any of these words you don't understand.

ancestor	curtain	moral	teddy bear
arthritis	dais	paradise	tennis outfit
astronauts	fan	personalities	testimonial
cafeteria	funeral	plaque	trademark
checkbook	honoree	swampland	widow
crib	miser	take-out	

3. PREVIEW THESE SENTENCES. Listen to the Preview Sentences for Unit Ten. Then fill in the missing words. You may check your answers on pages 153–154.

1. The best laughs of all were had at The Friars, a world-famous theatrical club in New York City where Joey Adams invited us to attend a special _____ dinner called a "roast."

2. And after we've all laughed ourselves sick over the insults directed at the guest of honor, the _____ then has an opportunity to _____ and respond to all that's been said.

3. "We really love each other—and if you believe that, I have some _____ in Jersey I'd like to _____ on you."

4. "_____ aren't fun to live with, but they make wonderful _____."

5. "My parents didn't want me—they put a live _____ in my _____."

6. "You can always tell a _____ in Beverly Hills. She wears a black _____."

Make sure you understand what the sentences mean before you continue.

Now, Let's Laugh

☼☼ Listen to the comedian. Then decide if the statements you hear in the middle of the monologue are true or false. You may check your answers on page 161.

Write your answers here.

1. Hawaii is the show-business capital of the world. _____

2. The Catskill Mountains is a resort area near New York City. _____

3. Only people who are hated are roasted. _____

4. Milton Berle became a comedian when his mother bought him a rocking chair. _____

5. The swampland that Johnny Carson talked about is valuable land in New Jersey. _____

Check Yourself

Listen to the comedian again before you do the exercises. When you have finished, check your answers on pages 161, 154, and 156.

1. COMPREHENSION CHECK. Answer each question with a sentence.

1. What is a "roast"? _____

2. How did the Friars Club get started? _____
   _____

3. What category does the joke about Milton Berle losing his marbles fall
   into? (ethnic, wordplay, put-down, or anticlimax) _____

4. What is Rodney Dangerfield's trademark? _____

5. Why did Woody Allen say his parents didn't want him? _____
   _____

6. What problems can cause comedians to lose their audience? _____
   _____

2. WHAT'S MISSING? Listen again, and complete the jokes.

The _____ _____ of all _____ _____ ____ The Friars, a

_____ theatrical _____ in _____ _____ _____, where

_____ Adams _____ us to _____ __ _____ testimonial _____

called a _____. _____ a roast? _____ a _____

_____ that honors a _____ in a _____ way—by

_____ _____ of him or her. And the _____, _____ is

_____ _____ for its _____ roast of

_____, raises _____ _____ _____ show-business

_____ and _____ other _____ _____. At these _____,

_____ by more _____ a _____ _____, there are

_____ _____ selected _____ sitting on the _____

_____ _____ entertainment ____ _____ for about five

_____ in a _____ _____ way. And after we've ____

_____ ourselves sick over the _____ _____ at the

116

_____ ___ _____, the honoree then _____ an _____ to _____ and respond to ___ _____ been _____.

Finally, Carl Reiner: "The _____ _____ up all _____ and looked _____ a _____. He _____ to his _____, 'I haven't _____ _____ all night _____ _____ afraid of my wife. She _____ I _____ _____ in my _____ last night _____ _____ _____ I was _____ to play _____, but _____ thought ____ was a 10-_____ game. Well, I _____ every _____—all $500— _____ I can't _____ her.' His _____ _____ sorry _____ him _____ _____ him the _____ and _____ him to go _____ _____ face his wife. He said, ' _____, pal. Can you ____ me _____ more _____? _____ you let me have _____ $100? I'd like to _____ her I _____ __ winner.' "

Follow It Up

1. WORKING TOGETHER. Write questions about the passage you just heard using vocabulary from this unit, and ask your partner to answer them. *Or* write a dialog together in which you discuss the different comedians you've seen and what you think of them.

_____

_____

_____

_____

_____

2. FINDING SYNONYMS. Answer each question with a sentence that uses a synonym from this unit for the underlined word or phrase.

1. What is the <u>symbol</u> for your company or your country? _____

_____

2. In your family, are there any <u>people who hate to spend money</u>? _____

_____

3. Did you just wander into this classroom? _____

_____

4. Do you often think about your relatives who came before you? _____

_____

5. When you were a baby, did you sleep in a baby bed? _____

_____

6. Would you have the strength to fight back if you were attacked? _____

_____

7. Do you know anybody who is crazy? _____

_____

8. If you wrote a book, how would you publicize it? _____

9. Did you ever try to get rid of something that you knew was worthless?

_____

10. Would you like to visit the place where they make television shows?

_____

3. COMPLETING SENTENCES. Fill in the blanks with words from this list.

cafeteria	producer	gullible	wouldn't be found dead in
sentimental	modestly	fan	personalities
press agent	funeral	plaque	worthy cause
honoree	take-out	handy	fund-raising

1. Helping poor people find jobs is a _____.

2. Are you _____ with a paintbrush? I need someone who knows how to paint.

3. This dress is so old that I _____ it.

4. Reggie has many _____ since he won the last tennis game. Everybody wants to talk to him.

5. You won't find gourmet cuisine here. All you can get is _____ food.

6. I wouldn't be a successful television star if I didn't have a good _____. She puts my name in print.

118

7. Let's not eat in the school _____ tonight. Let's go to a restaurant.

8. How could you believe that watch was worth $1,000? You are so _____.

9. I can see by the way you talk about your childhood that you're a _____ person. You really have deep feelings, don't you?

10. Many Americans cried as they attended the _____ for John F. Kennedy in 1963.

11. "Since I'm the _____ of this dinner, I'd like to thank you all for showing your appreciation of me."

12. This is a _____ event. We hope to collect at least $10,000 for cancer research.

13. Have you seen the _____ presented to Sarah as "Doctor of the Year"? She's going to hang it on her office wall.

14. Barbie accepted her trophy _____ even though she knew she truly deserved it.

15. The _____ of this show expect to lose a lot of money. The show will close at the end of this week.

16. The movie _____ of yesterday wll never be forgotten because their work is preserved on film.

Take It Further

1. Who are the funny people in your country? What makes them so funny—their material, their delivery, their appearance, or a combination?
2. In pairs or groups, name all of the comedy shows you can think of, including talk shows and situation comedies. Then name the funny American movies you've seen. Share your lists with the class.
3. What are your *favorite* American comedy shows—situation comedies, talk shows, etc.? Why do you like them? Focus on a single show, and describe the characters, the usual setting (time and place), and the typical story lines or themes.
4. Have you ever seen a roast? Would you enjoy being at one? Well, here is your opportunity to experience a roast for yourself. Choose a member of your class to roast, and do it with humor, of course. Then

let him or her respond to each of you, with humor, of course! If you are at a loss for a butt of jokes, use American humor. Roast American humor. Now that you have been immersed in it for weeks, what would you like to say?

5. Explain what is funny about the jokes you heard on the tape. Look at the tapescript for this unit, and discuss each of the jokes.

6. And for your final activity, "try your hand" (and imagination) at being a comedian. Write your own material.

    a. Pick a topic—like school or society. Then write down a list of associations—all the words that come to mind when you think of this topic.

    b. Write a statement about this topic with the association, using *so* or *such* and *that*. Be ironic or sarcastic, and exaggerate. (For example, "School is *so* exciting *that* I need an alarm clock in my desk to keep me awake." "The climate is *so* healthy in that town *that* they had to kill a man to start a cemetery." "The plane was *so* fast *that* it took off from Los Angeles with two rabbits and landed in New York with only two rabbits.")

Now It's Your Turn

1. Think of all the topics we covered in this book—family members, travel, professions, health, government and politics, marriage, etc.

2. Choose a topic, and then write down all the words that you associate with it.

3. Write a few funny lines related to this topic. Consider possible introductory phrases, transitional phrases, and concluding remarks.

4. Underline the words you want to stress, mark off the places where you should pause for dramatic effect before the punch line, and choose the appropriate intonation patterns.

5. Practice your delivery.

6. And "the floor is yours:"

Today, we are lucky to have _____,
                                                (stage name)

straight from the_____ **nightclub located**
                        (name of nightclub, hotel, or cafe)

in _____, _____. **And without any**
              (city)   (country)

further ado, here (he/she) is: _____!
                                              (stage name)

Tapescript

UNIT ONE, *The Delivery*, Part I

PREVIEW THESE SENTENCES

1. Jack, a new *inmate*, saw Wally, an old *con man*, walk up to a prisoner, call out "Number 25!" and walk away, leaving the prisoner laughing.

2. Words certainly contribute to the end result, but the *tone of voice*, the *stress*, the *pacing*, and everything else that *comprises* the delivery of a joke have the power to turn ordinary words into *catalysts* of laughter.

3. He might deliver it without any obvious emphasis and "throw it away" as if the words were unimportant, or he might use a *sarcastic* tone of voice or an accent and be even more successful.

4. Without the right *emphasis* and *inflection*, the joke will *bomb, fall flat on its face*, and die!

5. It gives the audience a chance to *digest* all the information they've heard; at the same time, it creates a little *suspense* as it *signals* that the *climax* is just about to come.

NOW, LET'S LAUGH

Here's another joke for you.

> It was lunch time and the prisoners were outside getting some air, Jack, a new *inmate*, saw Wally, an old *con man*, walk up to a prisoner, call out "Number 25!" and walk away, leaving the prisoner laughing. Next, he saw Wally walk up to another prisoner, call out "Number 6!" and again walk away, leaving the man laughing. After this happened several times, Jack went over to Wally and asked him what he said that made those prisoners laugh. Wally said he was telling them jokes, but, because they already knew the jokes, it was only necessary to call out the number of each joke.
>
> The next day Jack, thinking that he would make friends quickly by entertaining the prisoners, proceeded to do what he saw Wally do. He walked up to one inmate, called out "Number 25!" and waited for laughter. But none came. He walked over to another prisoner, called out "Number 6!" and again waited for laughter; again nothing happened. After he tried this several times, he walked over to Wally, told him what had happened, and asked him for advice. Wally, not wanting to hurt Jack's feelings but having no choice in the matter, told him, "Sorry, my friend, but it's all in the delivery; you have to know how to tell a joke!"

I hope you liked this joke and I hope you got the *message*. In the Introduction, we said the main ingredient in every good joke is a sudden alteration or change in point of view.

What we didn't say is something you've probably figured out by yourselves, and that is, the structure of a joke is only half of the *recipe*. Words certainly contribute to the end result, but the *tone of voice*, the *stress*, *the pacing*, and everything else that *comprises* the delivery of a joke have the power to turn ordinary words into *catalysts* of laughter. And as the joke you just heard suggests, even a number can make someone laugh if you say it right.

There are many different ways of delivering a line. A comedian can take a simple sentence and by delivering it with a certain *inflection* in his voice produce *peals of laughter*. He might deliver it without any obvious emphasis and "throw it away" as if the words were unimportant, or he might use a *sarcastic* tone of voice or an accent and be even more successful. He has choices, but not all types of deliveries are appropriate for all kinds of jokes. It takes a sensitive comedian to make the right choice. And those comedians who consistently choose the appropriate delivery are successful entertainers.

Let me show you how emphasis and other things can *make or break* a joke. Take the following joke, for example, and listen for the word that's stressed.

> "I can't stand him for another minute," Ethel screamed. "He gets drunk, spends all our money on *gambling* and other women, and if he comes home at all, it's just to change clothes."
>
> "It certainly looks like you have *grounds for divorce*," the lawyer said.
>
> "Divorce?" Ethel *hollered*. "I should say not! I've lived with that *bum* for thirty years. Now I should make him happy?"

Okay. What's the punch line? Right: "Now I should make him happy?" What word or words are stressed? If you said **now** and **happy**, you're correct. You can say this line many ways, but you'll usually get a laugh by stressing the words **now** and **happy**, by using a sarcastic tone of voice, and by finishing the line with rising *intonation* to make it a question. Without the right *emphasis* and *inflection*, the joke will *bomb, fall flat on its face*, and die!

By the way, I hope you remember that in spoken English you can change a statement into a question through rising intonation. For example, the statement "This is your book" can become a question if I say it this way: "This is your book?"

Enough review for now. Let's move to another example. Listen for wordplay in this one.

> "Mommy," said the little boy. "Are you still *burned up* about my *pranks*?"
>
> "Well," she said, "I guess I've *cooled down* a bit."
>
> "Well," he said, "you're gonna get burned up again. . . . I just set the living room on fire."

Did you notice the pause before the punch line, "I just set the living room on fire"? It's important because it serves a *dual* purpose. It gives the audience a chance to *digest* all the information they've heard; at the same time, it creates a little *suspense* as it *signals* that the *climax* is just about to come.

Frankly, even if the punch line is disappointing and not very funny, the audience is often so prepared to laugh that they do! Sometimes they laugh because they're embarrassed to admit they didn't get the joke, or they laugh to help the comedian *save face*. Whatever the reason, the point is that the right pacing, the right stress, and the right intonation can sometimes be enough to create laughter regardless of the words.

Listen to this next short joke and see what I mean.

> "Drinking makes you look beautiful."
> "I don't drink."
> "Ah, but I do!"

What a nice put-down joke! It works best if the words **I** and **do** are stressed in the punch line. If the words **do** or **but** are emphasized instead, the humor is lost.

Here's another one. Notice the words that are stressed in this joke.

His wife has just learned to drive the car, and now they are out in the *suburbs* racing along at eighty miles an hour. "Doesn't speeding over the beautiful country make you glad you're alive?" she asked.

"Glad?" He raised an eyebrow. "Glad isn't the word for it. I'm *amazed!*"

Did you notice that the words **glad** and **amazed** were both stressed? Did you also notice the pause before "I'm amazed"? Listen again if you didn't.

Now, if you are ready, listen to the following statements based on what you've heard, and decide whether they are true or false.

1. There is only one way to tell a joke.
2. The wrong emphasis can ruin a joke.
3. A joke is successful when it bombs.
4. Audiences often laugh because they don't want to admit they didn't understand the joke.

UNIT ONE, Part II

PREVIEW THESE SENTENCES
1. Pacing is the speed at which one speaks and the length and *frequency* of pauses separating units of thought.
2. The horse hugged the rail, the *jockey* had his hands around the horse's neck, and I . . . kissed my money goodbye.
3. A young *second lieutenant*, listening with *disgust, muttered* to the woman at his side, "What a *pompous* and *unbearable* old *windbag* he is."
4. It was in early 1962, on the day John Glenn became the first American to go into *orbit*, and the nation went wild over his *feat* of remaining in outer space for three *revolutions*.
5. The words count, but the delivery determines the *fate* of the joke.

NOW, LET'S LAUGH
Sometimes jokes are better when the teller is a good mimic—that is, the joke-teller can imitate other people's speech and behavior. Here's a joke in which a man imitates a woman's voice.

It was a beautiful day, and Fox didn't want to go to work. So he called his office and said, in a woman's voice, "Mr. Fox isn't feeling well and won't be coming in."

"Oh, I see," said the secretary. "And who's calling?"

"Er, this is my wife speaking," replied Fox.

That one should be funny in any society. But the most important ingredient in its delivery isn't the imitation of a woman's voice, but the pacing—particularly that little pause before the punch line. Do you know why? I'll give you a hint. During that pause, the man was thinking of what to say. Did he say the right thing? If you know the answer to that question, you understand the punch line. If not, listen carefully the next time you hear this joke.

Pacing is the speed at which one speaks and the length and *frequency* of pauses separating units of thought. Words can be spoken quickly or slowly, and sentences can be interrupted by pauses or followed by pauses. The speed at which comedians speak, the way they group their words, where they stop to pause, and how long they pause: all these things contribute to their delivery.

Listen to another joke, and notice where the pauses occur and the speed at which the joke is delivered. You should also be able to hear the words that are stressed.

It was a very *affectionate* race. The horse hugged the rail, the *jockey* had his hands around the horse's neck, and I . . . kissed my money goodbye.

It sure was a *romantic* race, though not very successful. Anyway, I hope you see what I mean about pacing.

The next joke also illustrates the importance of pacing. Pay close attention to all of the elements of the delivery—the stress, the tone of voice, the intonation, and, of course, the pacing. And at the same time, enjoy it.

> At a military *social function*, the commanding general of the base delivered a very long and boring speech. A young *second lieutenant*, listening with *disgust*, *muttered* to the woman at his side, "What a *pompous* and *unbearable* old *windbag* he is!"
>
> The woman turned to him at once and said, "Lieutenant, do you know who I am?"
>
> "No, ma'am," he said.
>
> "I am the wife of that unbearable old windbag, as you call him."
>
> "Indeed," said the young lieutenant, looking *stern*, "and do you know who I am?"
>
> "No, I don't," said the general's wife.
>
> "Well, thank God!" said the lieutenant, and he quickly disappeared.

If you like that joke, then you should like this next one. Listen, and while you do, think about the category in which it belongs.

> It was in early 1962, on the day John Glenn became the first American to go into *orbit*, and the nation went wild over his *feat* of remaining in outer space for three *revolutions*. The next day, Sara, still excited, said to her friend Becky, "What do you think of John Glenn?"
>
> Becky raised her eyebrows and said, "Who?"
>
> Sara, astonished at Becky's lack of knowledge, said, "John Glenn! John Glenn! He just went around the world three times!"
>
> Becky shrugged her shoulders. "Well," she said, "if you have the money, you can afford to travel."

How do you like that punch line? As usual, the joke works well if the right words are stressed, the voice rises and falls in the right places, and the punch line is delivered in a very casual way. In order for the punch line to be funny, it must be delivered in a casual, *nonchalant* manner that *reflects* Becky's indifference to this very unusual achievement. Because Becky *minimizes* the value of John Glenn's achievement, by making it sound as simple and *mundane* as taking a trip by plane, the joke is funny.

Well, here's one more joke for you to enjoy.

> For years, Jones had refused to take planes, and all arguments urging him to do so were made *in vain*. Finally one friend said in exasperation, "Listen, Jones, why don't you take a *philosophical* approach? Tell yourself that if *your number isn't up*, then it isn't up, and take the plane."
>
> "Ah," said Jones, "and what difference would it make if my number wasn't up, but the pilot's number was?"

Now what do you say to that? How would you answer that question? Think about it, and think about what I said before. The words count, but the delivery determines the *fate* of the joke. So the person who tells it can make all the difference in the world. In another unit, you will hear about many of the comic *geniuses* that keep America laughing.

Right now, I'd like you to listen to the following statements and decide whether they are true or false. By this time I'm sure you know where to write your answers. Here goes.

1. The man kissed his money because his horse won the race.
2. The lieutenant didn't realize he was talking to the general's wife.
3. Sara and Becky were both excited over John Glenn's achievement.
4. Fox stayed at home because his wife was sick.

UNIT TWO, *Introducing . . . The Professions!*, Part I

PREVIEW THESE SENTENCES
1. In fact, we often joke about our work or about someone else's profession, in order to *relieve* fear and *envy*.
2. I called my doctor the other day and told him I had taken an *overdose* of *aspirin*.
3. "Relax. It couldn't possibly be *appendicitis*. She probably has a touch of *indigestion*."
4. Doctors aren't the only professionals that get *worked over* by comedians.
5. So he found a lawyer who *advertised* that, for a $50 *retainer*, he could help anybody.

NOW, LET'S LAUGH
In America, our jobs and our professions are important to us, but like everything else, they too can become the butt of humor. In fact, we often joke about our work or about someone else's profession, in order to *relieve* fear and *envy*. Whom do we fear and envy most? Well, in the United States, the answer probably is doctors and lawyers.

The first joke shows why we fear doctors.

> A team of doctors stood around an elderly patient, who was being kept alive by machines. There was one machine that helped him breathe. Another kept his heart going, *electronically*. A third machine *pumped* his blood. And so on.
> Suddenly, the door flew open, and a nurse came running in, late. In her hurry, she *tripped* over the wires and pulled out all the plugs for the machines. "Hey!" cried one of the doctors. "Who turned off the patient?"

The punch line may sound like an exaggeration of what really exists in hospitals, but unfortunately it isn't. In some cases, people have been kept alive solely by an electronic support system. So while we may laugh at this joke, we probably do so out of fear.

What do you think the following joke is telling us about doctors?

> I called my doctor the other day and told him I had taken an *overdose* of *aspirin*. I said, "What do I do?" He said, "Take two aspirin and call me in the morning."

You see, doctors are sometimes so busy that, without thinking, they respond to a patient's *complaint* with the *routine* advice "Take two aspirin and call me later." This joke makes the doctor appear particularly *inept*, because he *obviously* didn't listen to the patient's problem. Aspirin was the worst thing he could have prescribed in this case.

> My friend, the *plumber*, was so disgusted with this kind of response that he *paid* his doctor *back* one day. The doctor had phoned and asked him to repair a *clogged-up* sink. "Tell you what, Doc," the plumber said. "Just put two aspirin in the sink, and I'll be over in a few hours to see how you're getting along."

I'll bet this doctor will think twice before *prescribing* aspirin again!

One more joke about doctors. Actually, there are so many good ones, it's hard to choose just a few. Anyway, here goes.

Mr. Jones hadn't called his doctor for several years. Now it was two o'clock in the morning, and his wife had a bad stomachache that he was sure was *appendicitis*. The doctor said, "Relax. It couldn't possibly be appendicitis. She probably has a touch of *indigestion*. I took out your wife's appendix ten years ago, and in all of medical history, I've never heard of anyone having a second appendix."

"That may be true," Mr. Jones said, "but haven't you ever heard of anybody having a second wife?"

I would think the punch line of this joke needs no explanation, but if it does, ask a friend, a teacher, or anyone else for help.

Doctors aren't the only professionals that get *worked over* by comedians. Lawyers get just about as much attention. Listen to this story.

Every time a certain *hostile witness* at a trial answered a question, he *preceded* his answer with "I think." When this happened a third time, the lawyer lost his *patience* and insisted that the witness tell the court and *jury* what he knew, not what he thought.

In response, the witness quietly said, "I'm not a lawyer; I can't talk without thinking."

I'd say that's one of the best put-downs I've heard in a long time. Wouldn't you agree?

Now listen to this one about another lawyer.

Harry, a businessman, had trouble collecting money from a customer. So he found a lawyer who *advertised* that, for a $50 *retainer*, he could help anybody. When Harry gave the lawyer the money, the lawyer said, "Thank you. This *entitles* you to two questions."

Harry said, "What! Fifty dollars for two questions! Isn't that very high?"

The lawyer replied, "Yes, I suppose so; now, what's your second question?"

Perhaps that joke exaggerates the *greed* of lawyers. But it was funny, wasn't it?

There are other professions we joke about, but let's stop here and decide whether the following statements are true or false.

1. People never joke about their own work, only about other people's work.
2. It's possible to keep people alive electronically.
3. Mr. Jones called his doctor because his wife had indigestion.
4. People fear and envy lawyers.
5. The joke about Harry and his lawyer shows the greed of businesspeople.

UNIT TWO, Part II

PREVIEW THESE SENTENCES

1. The phone rang at the firehouse just five minutes after the men had all *retired* for their afternoon *nap*.
2. Not even movie stars are *exempt* from jokes.
3. Here's one about a waiter who doesn't really know much about food preparation and takes his orders too *literally*.
4. I'm counting my money before you *give me the gas*.
5. So he went to see a man he'd once *befriended*—Bob Baker, the *realtor*—about renting a cheap building.

NOW, LET'S LAUGH

Fortunately for doctors and lawyers, no line of work is *sacred*. At one time or another, every kind of occupation has been under attack. Even the firefighter can't escape. Listen to this one.

> The phone rang at the firehouse just five minutes after the men had all *retired* for their afternoon *nap*. "There was a terrible blast at my house," a woman cried. "The flames are traveling through the basement and the first floor. Pretty soon they'll destroy the entire place."
> "Did you try throwing water over it?" asked the fire chief.
> "Yes!" cried the woman.
> "Then there's no use in our coming over. That's all we do."

Now that isn't exactly the kind of response you expected to get, is it?
Here's one about an *optometrist*.

> "You need glasses," said the optometrist.
> "I'm wearing glasses," said the patient.
> "Oh, then I need glasses."

Perhaps a doctor is the author of this next joke, about a plumber.

> An urgent call was put in for a plumber at noon, but he didn't arrive until eight hours later. "How is it?" he asked upon entering the house.
> "Not so bad," replied the homeowner. "While we were waiting for you to arrive, I taught my wife to swim."

Not even movie stars are *exempt* from jokes. Take this joke, for example.

> The handsome movie actor stopped the police officer and asked for directions. Then he waited for some sign of *recognition*, but none came. "Er-uh, don't you recognize me?" he asked the cop.
> "Sure, you're the fellow who's gonna buy that butcher shop on Seventh Avenue."
> "No, no," said the actor. "Haven't you seen me in films?"
> "Yes. And take my advice. Buy that butcher shop."

That wasn't very nice, now, was it? But to Americans, it's funny.
Here's one about a waiter who doesn't really know much about food preparation and takes his orders too *literally*.

> The man called the waiter to him and in a boisterous voice said, "I want a chicken *smothered in gravy*."
> "If you want it killed in a cruel way like that," said the waiter, "you'll have to do it yourself!"

And we mustn't forget a professional who is feared as much as the doctor. I'm speaking of the dentist, of course. The following joke shows that people don't always trust dentists.

> DENTIST: My good man, you don't have to pay me now, before I take out your tooth.
> PATIENT: Pay you? I'm counting my money before you *give me the gas*.

I'd say this patient doesn't trust this dentist. Wouldn't you agree?
And for our final joke on professions, here's one about a *calculating* businessperson.

> Max was a little *hard-pressed*; business was so bad he had to give up his expensive store, and his daughter married an honest but poor man. So he went to see a man he'd once *befriended*—Bob Baker, the *realtor*—about renting a cheap building.
> "I want $100 a month," said Bob. This *infuriated* Max, but he thought he'd show Baker up for the *cheap person* he was.

So he said, "I'll be more generous than you; I'll give you $125."

"I'm generous, too. You can have it for $75," said Baker.

"No, I'll give you $150," said Max.

"No, $50," said Baker.

"No," roared Max, "$175."

"No, no, no!" shrieked Bob Baker, *wizard* real-estate man. "I'll give it to you for nothing as long as I live."

"Make it as long as I live," said Max.

"Why?" asked Bob.

"Because," said Max, "I'm gonna take your *proposition*, and when I do, you're gonna drop dead."

Well, that's business for you.

If your profession, occupation, line of work, or job wasn't mentioned in these jokes, please don't be offended. Worse things could happen . . . like answering questions. Ready? These questions are different. Instead of answering "true" or "false," we want you to choose an appropriate statement. So listen to the first part of four statements. You will hear only the first part, the beginning. What you have to do is find the second part, the ending of the sentence, in your text. These endings will be listed next to the numbers 1 through 5. You even get an extra ending to make it more fun. Are you ready? Here goes.

a. A man went to see an optometrist because he _____.

b. The police officer's advice to the movie actor was to _____.

c. In the joke about the dentist, the patient _____.

d. Max, a businessman, raised his offer because Bob _____.

UNIT THREE, *Government and Politics*, Part I

PREVIEW THESE SENTENCES

1. Government leaders and politicians on all levels of government—local, state, and national—are *fair game* for comedians.

2. And even if we are not directly involved in the everyday *mechanics* of running our government, we have directly voted for the people who are.

3. Politicians are more likely to listen to humorous *criticism* than to bitter verbal *assaults*.

4. President Ronald Reagan, considered by friends and *foes* alike to be an excellent *communicator*, also used humor to its best advantage, especially during his last presidential campaign.

5. It's a program that was adopted in 1935 to ensure that *retiring* Americans would have money to live on.

6. In order to appreciate this joke, you have to know that children in America usually get at least one set of building blocks during their childhood and have great fun building different *structures*.

NOW, LET'S LAUGH

Listen to this joke.

> An old man was sitting on a park bench enjoying the late spring sunshine when another old man sat down at the other end of the bench. They viewed each other cautiously, and finally one of them heaved a tremendous heart-felt sigh. The other rose at once and said, "If you're going to talk politics, I'm leaving."

Now don't get any ideas. Yes, I am going to talk politics, but don't get up and leave, too. Speaking out against the government in many countries is forbidden or at least limited, but not here; in the United States, it's expected.

You won't go to jail for expressing your political opinion, but you can lose friends if you criticize their political party or bore them with your analysis of government affairs. Often the best way to get your point across is with a joke. Government leaders and politicians on all levels of government—local, state, and national—are *fair game* for comedians. In fact, many comedians concentrate much of their attention on what politicians are doing and not doing. Well-known *impressionists* have made careers out of *impersonating* U.S. presidents, vice-presidents, and other prominent national and international leaders.

Why are government and politics so popular among comedians? There are a few basic reasons. The government of the United States, both in theory and in practice, is made up of the people of the United States—its citizens. And even if we are not directly involved in the everyday *mechanics* of running our government, we have directly voted for the people who are. They represent us, and they're *accountable* to us. We can *criticize* them, *compliment* them, *hire* them, and *fire* them, and certainly we can joke about them.

We often joke about them to make a political point that people might not listen to if it were delivered in a serious manner. Politicians are more likely to listen to humorous *criticism* than to bitter verbal *assaults*. We also joke about them because they're in the *limelight*—in the news. They are the object of continuous *media coverage*. They provide topics most Americans who watch TV, listen to the radio, or read newspapers have common knowledge of.

Therefore, when someone tells a joke about what the President did today, for example, we can all laugh at it. Comedian Johnny Carson, the star and host of a very popular television program, "The Tonight Show," uses the news events of the day as material for his jokes. And you can be sure some newsmakers who are regular butts of humor on Johnny Carson's show are the President, members of Congress, and various government *bureaucrats*.

President Reagan, for example, was once criticized because he said Americans without food just didn't know where to get help. To make fun of that statement, Johnny Carson said Mr. Reagan should tell them to make their restaurant reservations a week in advance. Do you get it? What Mr. Carson is suggesting is that if you make your reservations well in advance, you'll get a table in the restaurant and you'll get food. But if you don't make your reservations well in advance, you may not get in. Of course, the suggestion itself is absurd, because if you don't have enough money for food, you certainly don't have enough money to spend at an expensive restaurant.

What you may find even more interesting is that the politicians themselves create some of the best jokes about themselves and their roles in government. As a matter of fact, many politicians use laughter as their greatest *weapon*, whether they're attacking or defending. And presidents, past and present, have been particularly skillful at this.

Take this story, which is told by the comedian, columnist, and author, Joey Adams.

> When a reporter asked John F. Kennedy, thirty-fifth President of the United States, how he could appoint his young brother, Bobby Kennedy, who was just out of law school, as the *attorney general* of the most powerful country in the world, Kennedy smiled and said, "Well, he's my kid brother, and I wanted to give him some experience before he opened his own law office."

Now if you analyze that answer, you will realize that the reason Mr. Kennedy gave for appointing his brother is ridiculous; nobody would seriously accept it. But Kennedy, rather than defend every move he made to every reporter who asked him a question, felt he would win greater support and make more friends by smiling and responding humorously and showing off his *keen wit* and his ability to handle situations.

President Ronald Reagan, considered by friends and *foes* alike to be an excellent *communicator*, also used humor to its best advantage, especially during his last presidential campaign. When Democrats and other *adversaries* suggested that Mr. Reagan was too old to run for President for a second *term*, comedians had a *field day* with jokes about Mr. Reagan's age. So did he!

Here's another story from Joey Adams.

> When I said, "Why do they say Reagan is too old to run for President just because his social security number is two?" Ronald Reagan called me personally. "Joey, this is Ron. What kind of *crack* is that about my age? I've got a funnier one. Why do they say I'm too old to be President just because my social security number is in *roman numerals*?"

In order to understand both of these jokes, you have to know something about the American social security system. It's a program that was adopted in 1935 to ensure that *retiring* Americans would have money to live on. As Americans enter the work world, they are given a social security number that remains with them the rest of their lives. Obviously, the older they are, the smaller their numbers should be. So the joke about Reagan's number being number two suggests that Reagan is extremely old. And Reagan's response that his number is in roman numerals suggests that he's as old as the Roman Empire.

But Reagan's feeling is, so what? Look how clever I am. And his thinking is, if I can show people I'm still witty, they'll forget about my age. And you know, his *strategy* worked. His wit and his delivery blinded many people to his age.

Here is another example of his humor.

> When Joey Adams told the President he had some political jokes for him, Reagan said, "I don't need them; I appointed plenty of my own."

Mr. Reagan's response is a good example of wordplay. Mr. Adams was talking about jokes—funny stories—but Reagan was using the term **joke** in a different sense. A joke can refer to something that is ridiculous, worthy of laughter rather than respect. And Mr. Reagan was specifically referring to people he had *appointed* who were now obviously *incompetent* officials.

The late Nelson Rockefeller, former Governor of New York and Vice-President of the United States, is also said to have had a great sense of humor. He laughed when Joey Adams said:

> "Rockefeller is a *self-made* man. His father had billions, but he treated Nelson like a normal kid. For Christmas he gave him a set of blocks— 50th Street, 51st Street, and 52nd Street."

In order to appreciate this joke, you have to know that children in America usually get at least one set of building blocks during their childhood and have great fun building different *structures*. You should also know that Nelson Rockefeller's father, John D. Rockefeller, Jr., was so wealthy he actually owned enough land for *genuine* city blocks to be carved from it. In fact, it's on land he *donated* to the United Nations in the heart of New York City that the *United Nations headquarters* was constructed in 1950. So you see, while normal children might *visualize* wood or plastic structures when they think of blocks, Nelson could easily have thought of land. Again, we have a play on words.

Lyndon Johnson, the vice-president who assumed the presidency when John F. Kennedy was *assassinated* in 1963, was also known for his sense of humor. According to Joey Adams, he got his biggest laughs when he was putting himself down. Remember those put-down jokes? Well, Lyndon Johnson once told Joey Adams to give him a big introduction before he delivered a speech at *Madison Square Garden* so that he could turn it into a joke. Here's the story as Adams tells it.

I introduced him at Madison Square Garden one night as the greatest President in the history of our country.

Johnson said, "My father would have loved that introduction, and my mother would have believed it. It's the greatest introduction I ever got. Except one time in Georgia, the governor was supposed to introduce me and he couldn't make it, so I introduced myself."

If you didn't get the jokes the first time around, don't worry. You'll have another chance. But right now, find out what you did understand by listening to the next few statements and deciding whether they are true or false.

1. Speaking out against the government is expected in the United States.
2. Politicians are more likely to listen to verbal assaults than to humorous criticism.
3. Johnny Carson is the host of a popular television show.
4. President Reagan got angry when people told jokes about his age.
5. Mr. Rockefeller got the United Nations headquarters for Christmas.

UNIT THREE, Part II

PREVIEW THESE SENTENCES
1. We can't help but admire, envy, and often respect people who are in the *spotlight* and *wield* power.
2. The media may ignore the good ones and tell us only about the ones who lie, cheat, and *embezzle*.
3. It is very *risky business* to ask a woman her age.
4. A sidewalk interviewer asked one of our *old-timers* what he thought of the two candidates for election.
5. "The Bible tells how the world was created out of *chaos*, and how could there be any order brought out of *chaos* without an engineer?"

NOW, LET'S LAUGH
Although we make fun of politicians, politics is actually a popular profession in the United States. We can't help but admire, envy, and often respect people who are in the *spotlight* and *wield* power. Even people who *fall from power* by abusing their positions still attract attention. For an example, listen to this next joke.

Politics is not a bad profession. If you succeed, there are many rewards. If you *disgrace* yourself or go to jail, you can always write a book.

How true! Believe it or not, there are numerous politicians who have shamed themselves and later *made a mint*. Look at former President Richard Nixon and members of his administration. After President Nixon, his attorney general, and several of his advisors left office because of the *Watergate scandal*, they wrote books and television scripts; some of these works were even written in jail. Later they made money and received much *publicity* by selling their work on television and giving lectures to large audiences across the country.

Now don't get me wrong. There are many excellent, *trustworthy* politicians in America. The dishonest ones, however, usually make more *sensational* news. The media may ignore the good ones and tell us only about the ones who lie, cheat, and *embezzle*.

In spite of the seriousness of this matter of official dishonesty, it's really difficult for politicians to be honest. They have to make many promises to many people. In view of this background information, I think you can figure out the next joke.

"I've been elected," the successful candidate excitedly telephoned his wife.

"Honestly?" replied the wife.

"Now why go into that?"

I'll give you a hint. There is a play on words; the husband and wife use one word in two different ways. See if you can figure out which word it is. The word is **honestly**. The wife used it to mean "really, are you joking?" and she said it like this: "Honestly?" And the husband *interpreted* **honestly** as "fairly, without cheating." Listen again to the whole joke to see how it was done.

"I've been elected," the successful candidate excitedly telephoned his wife.

"Honestly?" replied the wife.

"Now, why go into that?"

The next joke requires some background about American women. In America, there are certain topics that are *sensitive*, one being age. It is very *risky business* to ask a woman her age. Most likely she won't give you a *straight answer*. Based on this information, see if you can appreciate the punch line.

No woman is likely ever to be elected President; she will never reach the required legal age.

If you still need some help, let me add that, in order to become President of the United States, you must be at least 35 years old. And if women will never admit their age, we'll never know if they're *eligible* for the job. Now do you get it?

Try this next joke, and see how you do.

A sidewalk interviewer asked one of our *old-timers* what he thought of the two candidates for election.

"When I look at them," he said sorrowfully, "I'm thankful only one of them can get elected."

Why did the old-timer say that? Well, ask yourself: "What does he think of both candidates?" Not much! Right? Unfortunately, citizens sometimes feel that way about an election. In many cases, no choice—Democrat, Republican, or Independent—is satisfactory.

For another example, listen to the following joke, and see how an elderly woman feels about her choices.

During his speech, a politician noticed an elderly woman in the audience who appeared particularly interested in what he said. Afterwards, he took occasion to meet her and ask for her vote.

"Well, sir," the old lady said, looking him in the eye, "you're my second choice."

The politician thanked her and asked cheerfully, "And who is your first choice?"

"Oh," she replied, "just about anybody."

Here's one more joke that *reflects* how many people feel about politicians.

A doctor, an engineer, and a politician were arguing which of their professions was the oldest. The doctor said, "Of course, medicine is the oldest. Mankind has always had *physicians*, and they are even mentioned in the Bible."

"That's nothing," said the engineer. "The Bible tells how the world was created out of *chaos*, and how could there be any order brought out of *chaos* without an engineer?"

"Wait a minute," said the politician. "Who do you think created the chaos?"

And the answer is . . . ? Yes, indeed, politicians. Now remember, we could say good things about them, but you know that wouldn't have been funny.

Well, we'll give all politicians a rest for a while and let you get to work. Listen to the following statements and decide whether they are true or false.

1. Politicians who have fallen from power never make any money.

2. When you ask an American woman her age, she probably won't give you a *straight answer*.

3. In the joke about the candidate who was elected and called his wife, the word that the husband and wife used differently was **honestly**.

4. To be President of the United States, you must be at least 35 years old.

UNIT FOUR, *Members of the Family*, Part I

PREVIEW THESE SENTENCES

1. In fact, stand-up comedians—those people who literally stand up in front of audiences and tell jokes—spend at least half of their routines on their *spouses*, children, brothers, mothers-in-law, and other interesting relatives like lazy cousins, *unemployed* uncles, or *spinster* aunts.

2. One way they embarrass us is by *naively* saying anything that *pops* into their minds, *regardless* of how it sounds or whether it is appropriate.

3. The kids were *boasting* about their *respective* fathers.

4. Well, you should know that in America many parents are reluctant to discuss *"the birds and the bees"*—that is, sexual relationships.

5. Yes, indeed, *precocious* children like Stacy often surprise their parents with their knowledge and their powers of reasoning.

NOW, LET'S LAUGH

Welcome to our home. Come right in and meet the members of our family—each and every one a butt of humor. Yes, indeed, family members and their relationships provide more material than any one comedian can handle. In fact, stand-up comedians—those people who literally stand up in front of audiences and tell jokes—spend at least half of their routines on their *spouses*, children, brothers, mothers-in-law, and other interesting relatives like lazy cousins, *unemployed* uncles, or *spinster* aunts. We can't cover them all in one lesson, but we will try to give you a feeling for our family. Perhaps you'll recognize some of them one day, when you see them nearby or hear jokes about them.

Let me introduce our children first. No matter how good children may be, they get into trouble now and then and embarrass their parents. One way they embarrass us is by *naively* saying anything that *pops* into their minds, *regardless* of how it sounds or whether it is appropriate. They may say, for example, that a person looks old or fat or ugly, which is impolite in the American *code of etiquette*. They're also very skillful at "spilling the beans"—that is, telling their parents' secrets. Listen to the first joke and see what I mean.

> When the hero in the play slapped the heroine, a small voice in the audience was heard to ask, "But, Mom, why doesn't she hit him back like you do?"

I expect Mom was a little embarrassed.

In the next story, the joke is on Dad, not Mom. Let's listen to Paul "spill the beans."

> The kids were *boasting* about their *respective* fathers. "My daddy bathes twice a week," said Henry.
>
> "That's nuttin," said Allan. "My daddy bathes three times a week."

"Oh yeah?" said little Paul, not wishing to be outdone. "My daddy keeps himself so clean, he never has to take a bath."

Now, if you know anything about Americans in the United States, you know that most of them believe the saying, *"Cleanliness is next to godliness."* We believe in bathing often. Paul's father probably bathes once a day, but Paul, not yet aware of the importance of washing in our culture, will say anything to *outdo* the others. And as a result, he has provided a good laugh for the neighborhood.

Fortunately, as children mature and learn about their culture and the behavior that people expect, they make fewer mistakes of this kind, which we call *faux pas.* In fact, they become skillful at making clever remarks and manipulating adults.

Take Danny, for example. He was sitting on Santa Claus's lap, as many children do before Christmas, telling Santa what presents he wanted. (By the way, Santa Claus is a special person who lives at the North Pole and brings all the presents on Christmas Eve.) Normally, Santa would open his special book, which would tell him how well or badly the child had behaved during the year, and he would then write down what presents the child should receive. Let's see how well Danny did.

Danny said, "I want a train, a gun, an *erector set*, a chemistry set, a cowboy suit, a bicycle, a *catcher's mitt*, a *transformer*, a set of soldiers, a toy garage with cars and trucks, and a mini-television."

"Okay," laughed Santa. "I'll look in the book and see if you were a good boy."

"Ah, never mind looking in the book. I'll settle for a pair of *roller skates.*"

Good thinking. If Santa had looked in his book and noticed all the times Danny misbehaved, Santa wouldn't have brought him anything. Very clever that Danny.

Now I'll introduce you to other children who are equally smart, children who put their parents to the test by asking very challenging questions and by not accepting answers that don't make sense or that can't be proven. For an example, listen to this next joke.

ALEX: Mom, where did that baby come from?
MOM: Why, the *stork* brought him, Alex, and he's your baby brother. Would you like to see him?
ALEX: Nah, I wanna see the stork.

What's funny about that joke? Well, you should know that in America many parents are reluctant to discuss *"the birds and the bees"*—that is, sexual relationships. So they tell their children that large birds called storks deliver babies. Naturally, Alex would rather see this incredible stork that brought his baby brother than this baby who will only get in his way. And I can understand that. I'd want to see the stork, too.

Here's another joke about a child who is really too smart for the kinds of answers her mother gives.

A seven-year-old girl, Stacy, asked her mother: "Mom, where did I come from?"

The mother replied, "The stork brought you."

"Where did *you* come from?" asked the girl.

"The stork brought me too."

"And Grandma?"

"The stork brought Grandma, too."

"That's funny," said Stacy. "We haven't had a normal birth in our family in three generations."

134

Yes, indeed, *precocious* children like Stacy often surprise their parents with their knowledge and their powers of reasoning. Consequently, many parents get worn out by their children. As much as they love them, they're glad to send the kids off to school so that teachers can answer their questions. And in the summer, parents are quite happy to send their children off to *day camp*, or *sleep-away camp*, where they can play and work off their excess energy. One parent put it this way.

> I always look forward to summer camp. I'm one of those parents who find that school runs out just about the time my patience does.

But as difficult as young children may be, teenagers cause the most problems in *parenting*. They question their parents' authority, rebel at society's rules, and don't clean their rooms or do anything else around the house because they're too busy talking on the phone. The next joke reflects this situation.

> Children grow up so quickly—one day you look at the phone bill and realize they're teenagers.

When they're not talking on the phone, they're often debating something with their parents—their homework, their grades, using the family car, staying out late and, would you believe it, even keeping clean!

Another joke about teenagers goes this way.

> There's a brand-new *scent* that's driving teenagers out of their minds. They've never experienced anything like it. It's called **Clean**!

And speaking of clean, let's make a clean break and give our children a rest while you answer a few true-or-false questions. Then we will turn our attention to their parents.

1. When children "spill the beans," they get dirty.
2. Stand-up comedians could spend at least half of their routines on their families.
3. Santa tells children what he'll bring them when they sit on his lap.
4. Many parents find it difficult to discuss "the birds and the bees" with their children.
5. Precocious children often ask very challenging questions.

UNIT FOUR, Part II

PREVIEW THESE SENTENCES
1. She wants her daughter to *come out of the clouds*, take off her *rose-colored glasses*, and evaluate her fiancé in terms of his qualifications as a *wage earner*.
2. This is one of the reasons for the unpleasant *reputation* that mothers-in-law share.
3. Sometimes when Mother gets into her car, she's so *disoriented* that she has to think for a minute about where she's going.
4. There are many families that actually have *rogues* and failures who are butts of family jokes.
5. Among them was his *ne'er-do-well* nephew, who was the *black sheep* of the family.

NOW, LET'S LAUGH
Mothers are often criticized for being too possessive. Some mothers, it seems, want nothing more than to be the centers of their children's worlds, even if the effect on their children isn't positive. The following joke demonstrates this kind of thinking.

Mrs. Cohen was bursting with pride. "Did you hear about my son Louis?" she asked Mrs. Taylor.

"No. *What's with* your son Louis?"

"He's going to a *psychiatrist*. Twice each week he goes to a psychiatrist."

"Is that good?"

"Of course, it's good. Forty dollars an hour he pays. Forty dollars! And all he talks about is me."

I think the punch line is *self-explanatory*.

The next joke is about a mother trying to protect her daughter from romantic ideas of marriage.

Mother and daughter were arguing violently over daughter's selection of a *fiancé*. "But, Mother," she cried, "he said he'd put the *earth at my feet.*"

"My darling," Mother said, calming down, "you already have the earth at your feet. What you'll be needing is a roof over your head."

What do you think the mother is concerned about? Right: the fiancé's ability to provide a good home for her daughter. She's not concerned about the earth at her daughter's feet, because the young woman is already walking on the earth. She wants her daughter to *come out of the clouds*, take off her *rose-colored glasses*, and evaluate her fiancé in terms of his qualifications as a *wage earner*. This kind of attitude is typical of both parents when their daughters consider marriage. They want to know the answers to questions like: How will they live? What kind of a husband will their son-in-law be? Will he earn a good income, or will she have to support him?

It's interesting, however, that what some mothers want for their daughters, they don't necessarily want for their daughters-in-law. Listen to this next joke, and see what I mean.

Mrs. Botnick and Mrs. Gordon hadn't met in years. "Tell me," asked Mrs. Botnick, "what happened to your son?"

"My son—what a *misfortune!*" wailed Mrs. Gordon. "He married a girl who doesn't lift a finger around the house. She can't cook, and she can't sew a button on a shirt; all she does is sleep late. My poor boy brings her breakfast in bed, and all day long she stays there, *loafing.*"

"How terrible," said Mrs. Botnick. "And what about your daughter?"

"Ah, my daughter!" exclaimed Mrs. Gordon. "She married a man, an *angel*! He won't let her set foot in the kitchen. He gave her a full-time *maid* and a cook, and every morning he brings her breakfast in bed! And he makes her stay in bed all day."

This is what we call a *double standard*. What's good for her daughter should be good for her daughter-in-law, but in many families it doesn't work that way. This is one of the reasons for the unpleasant *reputation* that mothers-in-law share.

Men as fathers and fathers-in-law aren't treated as badly in jokes, perhaps because they don't usually get as involved in the daily activities of the family members. But as husbands, they are frequently *roasted*. Notice how husbands are shown in television comedies. They appear to misunderstand their children and make a terrible mess when they do something around the house. There are very pointed jokes about men as husbands who don't understand how hard it is to do housework. For an example, listen to this joke about a *spoiled* husband who doesn't appreciate what he's got.

The husband lectured his wife: "Stick to your washing, ironing, *scrubbing*, and cooking. No wife of mine is going to work."

I'm sure you've heard of the *women's liberation movement*, but apparently this husband hasn't. It's *ironic* that he thinks she doesn't work, when she does so many hard *chores*.

Another chore that mothers are constantly called upon to do is *chauffeur* their children to different places. The weekly schedule gets very hectic. Sometimes when Mother gets into her car, she's so *disoriented* that she has to think for a minute about where she's going. Listen to this next joke, and you'll *get the picture*.

> Kids *have it made*. Their mothers drive them everywhere. They drive them to school, to their friends' homes, to the movies, to the *bowling alley*, and to dancing lessons. I know one kid who wanted to *run away* from home, and his mother said, "Wait, I'll drive you."

I'm sure she didn't mean it. Or did she?

Well, let's give Mom a rest now and listen to a few jokes about other members of our family tree—some members that are not so impressive. For example, there are Jack's aunt and uncle, who are in the iron and steel business: She does the ironing, and he does the stealing. Although what you just heard was a joke, there are many families that actually have *rogues* and failures who are butts of family jokes and sometimes cause much embarrassment. Here's a joke that shows the point.

> Jones discovers that Brown has been having his family tree studied, and he asks Brown about it. "Yeah," says Brown, "I've spent $5,000 altogether."
>
> "Well," says Jones, "I guess it's pretty expensive to look up a family tree."
>
> "It cost me only $2,000 to have it looked up," replied Brown. "The other $3,000 was to have it hushed up."

See what I mean about people being sensitive about the members of their family?

Most people won't pay to have their relatives kept hidden, but on the other hand, they may simply pretend not to know them in public. And they most certainly will omit them from their *wills*. Speaking of wills, listen to our final joke in this unit, which is about a family who has come to a will-reading to hear how their dead relative has divided up his money and possessions.

> After the rich man's funeral, the family gathered in the library to hear his lawyer read his will. Among them was his *ne'er-do-well* nephew, who was the *black sheep* of the family. The lawyer read the *bequests* to the rich man's wife, his daughter, his sister, and on and on. Then the lawyer cleared his throat.
>
> "And finally, to my nephew, Alan, who has been so *attentive* to me during my final illness, who said he considered himself the son I never had, and who once *subtly* reminded me to mention him in my will: To you, Alan"—here Alan eagerly stood up, waiting to hear his reward—"I'd like to say, 'Hello there; how nice of you to come!'"

Poor Alan. I think he wanted to be mentioned in a different way. He certainly didn't get what he came for, like money or other valuables.

But that's not your problem. You have other things to think about, like the answers to the following true-or-false questions.

1. When Louis visits his psychiatrist twice a week, he talks about his mother.
2. Mothers want the same things for their daughters and daughters-in-law.
3. Mothers spend a lot of time driving their chauffeurs different places.
4. In jokes, fathers are treated just as badly as mothers.
5. Family black sheep are usually mentioned in wills.

UNIT FIVE, *Marriage, Cheating, and Divorce*, Part I

PREVIEW SENTENCES

1. And though some marriages may resemble a three-ring circus, with its *frantic* activity, the comparison is made in jest.

2. To help you avoid embarrassment, we're going to give you practice identifying the *advent* of a joke by omitting, from time to time, our formal announcement that "the following is a joke."

3. After all, what can we expect when two different people with different backgrounds and *idiosyncrasies* get together and try to live under the same roof, supposedly forever?

4. Then there was this *drunk* who was brought into *night court*, having been picked up on *suspicion* of being the *notorious* night *prowler*.

5. It *raged* far into the night, and finally she couldn't take it any more, so she *adopted* the position of *"peace at any price."*

NOW, LET'S LAUGH

> Love is a three-ring circus.   Engagement ring, wedding ring, and suffer-ing.

Do you think we mean this?   Do you think we are seriously telling you that love makes people suffer?   No, of course not.   You've just heard a joke that plays on the word **ring**.   There are rings that engaged and married people wear, and there are circles called rings in which circus performers and *acrobats* all perform at the same time.   And though some marriages may resemble a three-ring circus, with its *frantic* activity, the comparison is made in jest.

How are you supposed to know you've heard a joke if you haven't been formally warned?   Well, you should listen and watch for certain clues that are usually *reliable*.   Often the speaker smiles or speaks in a playful or sarcastic tone of voice.   Or the speaker begins the joke about a person or topic in very general terms, like "Marriage is" or "Divorce is" or "Having children is *such and such.*"   Or perhaps the speaker starts talking about people you don't know.   For example: "Joe and Sue were married for two years" or "They were married for two years" or "This man and woman were married for two years."

Who are Joe and Sue?   Who are "they"?   You don't know.   They are *anonymous* people who work well in this joke.   If you did know them, the joke might be too painful or insulting to be funny.

The introductory words usually tell you when a joke is coming.   Special expressions include "Did you hear about the guy who . . . " or "Take the man who . . . " or "Like the woman who . . . " or "There was this kid who . . . ." One popular jokester uses the line "Take my mother-in-law—go on, take her!" What does it mean?   At the beginning of the sentence, **take** is supposed to mean "for example."   But the punch line, "take her," shows **take** in its more usual meaning.

If you're wondering why we've chosen this particular unit to review certain information on the delivery and structure of a joke, the reason is simple. Jokes that focus on the negative aspects of marriage and divorce are very common in America, and they may be easily misinterpreted, misunderstood, or missed altogether by people who come from cultures where these topics are never treated lightly.   To help you avoid embarrassment, we're going to give you practice identifying the *advent* of a joke by omitting, from time to time, our formal announcement that "the following is a joke."   And we suggest you listen even more closely now to see if you can tell when you are hearing fact or fiction or a combination.

Are you ready?   Now that you've been warned, let's get back to love—the *indescribable* feeling that encourages people to marry in spite of their fear. Why, you may ask, do people fear marriage?   Listen to all of our jokes on marriage and divorce, and you'll understand. Take this *client* who was telling his lawyer about his forthcoming marriage.

> "I'd like to congratulate you," said the lawyer. "You will always look back on this day as the happiest in your life."
>
> "Thank you," the man replied, "but it's tomorrow that I'm to be married."
>
> "Yes," said the lawyer, "I know. That's why I said what I did."

What's funny? If taken seriously, nothing! This joke presents the negative view of marriage. Why do people tell these jokes? Some people may tell them because they really aren't happy about marriage. Others, who are happily married, may tell such jokes because they feel society expects them to. Or perhaps they're *superstitious* and don't want to admit their happiness for fear they'll spoil it.

But no matter how good the marriage is, there are bound to be problems. After all, what can we expect when two different people with different backgrounds and *idiosyncrasies* get together and try to live under the same roof, supposedly forever? It takes two people who are willing to compromise, sacrifice, and share the responsibilities, like my friends, the Baumanns. The Baumanns had an outstandingly happy and successful marriage, and Mr. Baumann was once asked what the reason was.

> "It's simple," he said. *Division of labor.* I make all the big decisions, and my wife makes all the small, routine decisions. She decides what house we buy, where we go on vacation, whether the kids should go to private schools, if I should change my job, and so on."
>
> "And you, Mr. Baumann? What kind of decisions do you make?"
>
> "I don't know," he said. "The big decisions haven't come up yet."

Apparently, in the Baumann home, the wife *rules the roost*. What Mr. Baumann is really saying is that he makes no decisions at all that affect his family. For him, that may be okay. Many Americans believe that, in the home, the wife should be in charge.

Then there was this *drunk* who was brought into *night court*, having been picked up on *suspicion* of being the *notorious* night *prowler*.

> The judge sternly asked, "What were you doing out at 3 A.M.?"
>
> "I wash going to a lecture."
>
> "A lecture at 3 A.M.?" the judge asked skeptically.
>
> "Oh, sure," said the drunk. "Shometimes my wife shtays up later than that."

I can just imagine what this man's wife will say at this so-called "lecture"! What would you say?

There are other couples who share the power and work things out as equals. Take this couple.

> They were having a terrible battle. It *raged* far into the night, and finally she couldn't take it any more, so she adopted the position of *"peace at any price."*
>
> "I was wrong," she repeated. "Now, does that satisfy you?"
>
> "No!" he shouted. "You must admit that I was right!"

Have you ever heard or taken part in a similar conversation? If you haven't, you are one of the few. Many Americans, particularly marriage partners, like to be right and, even more important, like to get credit for being right.

However, there are still those who find arguing a waste of time, as long as they get what they want in the end. Consider the wife in this situation.

> The husband asked his wife angrily. "Another new hat!? Another new *fur*?! Where will we get the money to pay for them?"
>
> "Whatever my faults, dear," she answered, "I'm not *inquisitive*."

Isn't that nice? She doesn't question him about how the bills will be paid. She just expects them to be paid. How *convenient*!

Let's take a peaceful break and see how you're doing before we continue our gentle attack on marriage. For now, let's attack some true-or-false questions.

1. If a person smiles, he or she may be telling a joke.
2. People from certain cultures may misinterpret jokes about marriage and divorce.
3. Love can discourage people from marrying.
4. Only people who have bad marriages joke about marriage.
5. American men always rule inside the home.

UNIT FIVE, Part II

PREVIEW SENTENCES

1. "I consider that *accusation* wildly *absurd*," shouted the outraged Adam.
2. There, *hovering* over him, was Eve *painstakingly* counting his *ribs*.
3. According to the Bible, God created Adam, the first man, in His own *image*.
4. In fact, couples are actually signing *prenuptial* agreements that state how their *estate* will be divided up in the event of a divorce.
5. Divorce is so *prevalent* in Hollywood that families often can't keep track of who belongs and who doesn't.

NOW, LET'S LAUGH

In spite of the fact that an amazingly large number of wives work outside the home today and can pay for their own purchases, husbands are still concerned about the bills their wives run up while shopping. For example:

> I met this friend in the lobby of the Hilton hotel in Hong Kong. "My wife is an hour late," he growled. "She's either been *kidnapped*, hit by a car, or gone shopping. . . ." He shook his head. "I hope she hasn't gone shopping."

You should know what you've just heard was a joke. What *decent* husband would rather have his wife hit by a car or kidnapped than have her out shopping? The exaggeration in this joke should certainly have *clued you in*. Even people who have been hurt by their spouses have rarely wished them such a tragic ending.

But cheaters—that is, wives or husband who have *extramarital* affairs—come very close to being wished the worst. And cheating isn't exactly new. In fact, it may have started with the first couple mentioned in the Bible.

> Coming home very late one night, Adam found Eve waiting angrily. "Late again," she *pouted*. "You must be seeing some other woman."
> "I consider that *accusation* wildly *absurd*," shouted the outraged Adam. "You know perfectly well that you and I are quite alone in this world."
> With this, Adam retired for the night. But something soon caused him to awake with a start. There, *hovering* over him, was Eve *painstakingly* counting his *ribs*.

Those of you who are unfamiliar with the Bible will need some background information to appreciate what you've just heard. Here's your lesson for today. It's very simple, really. According to the Bible, God created Adam, the first man, in His own *image*. Then God created Eve, the first woman, from one of Adam's ribs. So if Eve had found another of Adam's ribs missing, what conclusion would she have come to? You got it! Another woman.

Here's another joke about cheating.

> Morris was awakened at 4 A.M. by his wife, who asked him, "If I were to die, would you get married again?"
> "What a question at this time of the morning," he mumbled.

> "Would you get married again?" she insisted.
>
> "Yeah," he admitted. "I suppose so. Eventually."
>
> "Would you bring her to live here in this house?"
>
> "This is a ridiculous conversation," he protested *drowsily*, "but it's a nice house, so why shouldn't we live here?"
>
> "Would you give her my car?"
>
> The husband yawned. "Why not? It's a *BMW*, and it's less than a year old. Yeah, I'd give her your car."
>
> "What about my golf clubs?"
>
> "No," Morris replied firmly. "I wouldn't give her your golf clubs."
>
> "Why not?"
>
> "Because," he said, "she's left-handed."

It seems Morris' wife finally found out what she didn't really want to know—that her husband was, indeed, cheating. And cheating is a very serious matter that often leads to divorce.

Did you hear the one about the husband who told the judge that he wanted a divorce because his wife called him a *lousy* lover?

> "You want a divorce just because your wife called you a lousy lover?" asked the judge.
>
> "No," he said. "I want a divorce because she knows the difference."

And how does she know the difference? Probably because she's been cheating. And so another marriage ends in divorce.

> Because there are so many divorces these days, they're making wedding rings lighter and thinner. In the old days, they were meant to last a lifetime.

What you just heard was another joke. It was delivered in a serious, matter-of-fact manner, but if you analyze the content, you'll realize that what I said is ridiculous. Why should the number of divorces affect the weight and size of wedding rings?

In reality, people don't think about divorce when they buy their wedding rings. What they do think about is what might happen to their money and their possessions should something go wrong with their marriage. In fact, couples are actually signing *prenuptial* agreements that state how their *estate* will be divided up in the event of a divorce. This sounds very cold and *calculating*, doesn't it? But people take this precaution in order to protect themselves and their fiancés from the financial ruin and the additional *grief* that can accompany a divorce.

> This one Hollywood mother was advising her daughter before the wedding ceremony. "Don't worry, dear," she said. "Mother will tell you everything you should know before you get married."
>
> The bride shrieked with delight. "That's wonderful! Then I'll be able to get as much *alimony* as you did."

Divorce is so *prevalent* in Hollywood that families often can't keep track of who belongs and who doesn't.

> Like the time the teacher told the actress's son to have his mother come to school next month.
>
> "I can't tell her," the boy said.
>
> "Don't you know where she's going to be next month?"
>
> "I don't even know *who* she's going to be next month."

Really, these jokes do exaggerate. Most people, even in Hollywood, genuinely hope that their love and marriage will last. Don't let these jokes turn you into a *cynic*. The state of marriage has been undergoing change since the beginning of time—since Adam and Eve. But it has survived and will probably last forever. Love certainly will.

On that happy note, let's make peace and relax with your true-or-false questions.

1. People who have extramarital affairs cheat on their spouses.
2. Comedians even use the Bible as a source for jokes.
3. Adam was created from Eve's rib.
4. Wedding rings are being made thinner because there are so many divorces.
5. Some people sign prenuptial agreements to prevent a divorce.

UNIT SIX, *Ethnic Humor,* Part I

PREVIEW THESE SENTENCES
1. This belief can be found even in the United States, which has always opened its doors to *immigrants* and is considered the largest *melting pot* in the world.
2. Try to remember that these jokes are only *caricatures* of the *minorities;* no race, creed, or color has the corner on *dum-dums,* and any joke about one group of people can be easily applied to another.
3. The *bulletproof vest* is to protect yourself from being hurt; you'll need imagination and sense of humor for obvious reasons, and your pen to fill in the *blank* spaces that would normally contain the name of an ethnic group but which we have omitted in cases where the joke might be considered *abusive.*
4. Did you hear about the "blank" scientist who developed an *artificial* appendix?
5. We can be real *hypocrites,* complaining about problems we ourselves created.

NOW, LET'S LAUGH

When Christopher Columbus, the Italian *explorer* sailing for Spain in 1492, landed on our shores, he hollered, "Hello, all you Americans!" And one Indian said to another, "Well, there goes the neighborhood."

How typical! Some people believe that the arrival of others from a different background or culture will make things worse in their community. This belief can be found even in the United States, which has always opened its doors to *immigrants* and is considered the largest *melting pot* in the world. For various social and economic reasons, the people already settled have often treated newcomers *initially* as intruders. It seems to be a natural protective response for people who are basically afraid of change. And one way people have of dealing with their fears is by joking about the so-called intruders. Hence, we have ethnic humor.

The jokes can be painful, particularly if your race, nationality, or religion is this year's target. Many people actually turn their heads or leave the room to avoid hearing people made fun of or criticized in this way. However, we would be *remiss* to omit ethnic jokes in this class. They exist, and they're not going away. New jokes are created all the time about the new person on the block.

So don't you go away. Take the advice of Joey Adams, the world-famous comedian whose book, *Ethnic Humor,* has provided us with many of our jokes: Try to remember that these jokes are only *caricatures* of the *minorities;* no race, creed, or color has the corner on *dum-dums,* and any joke about one group of people can be easily applied to another.

If you're ready, we will begin our unpredictable journey. Bring your *bulletproof vest,* your imagination, your terrific sense of humor, and a pen. The *bulletproof vest* is to protect yourself from being hurt; you'll need your imagination and sense of humor for obvious reasons, and your pen to fill in the *blank* spaces that would normally contain the name of an ethnic group but which we have omitted in cases where the joke might be considered *abusive*. Now if you understood that, get ready to have some fun and choose your own butts of humor—silently—when you hear the word *blank*.

Did you hear about the "blank" scientist who developed an *artificial* appendix?

Boy, is that scientist dumb! Why? Well, just think. What serious scientist would spend time and money developing a *substitute* for an *organ* that people can easily live without? Surely, no scientist I know.

What about the "blank" man who opened his lunch box every day and found a *peanut butter sandwich*? Each time he threw it away hollering, "I hate peanut butter sandwiches!"

After watching this for five days in a row, his co-worker asked, "If you don't like peanut butter sandwiches, why not tell your wife not to make peanut butter sandwiches?"

"What wife?" the "blank" man screamed. "I make my own sandwiches."

Obviously a very bright man! I guess he's afraid of changes of any kind, even those that would definitely be for the better.

The next joke shows that "blanks"—and here I mean any of us—sometimes speak without listening to what they say. If they heard themselves, they'd bite their own tongues.

The "blank" man went home and complained to his wife. "I saw Howard Smith downtown this morning and he didn't even speak to me. I guess he thinks I'm not his equal."

His wife responded, "Why, that stupid, brainless, *conceited*, good-for-nothing Howard Smith. You certainly are his equal!"

Thanks for the compliment! If this man's wife realized that, indirectly, she was saying that her husband was stupid, brainless, and conceited like Howard Smith, she probably would have *apologized*. In any case, we don't need two stupid good-for-nothings walking around.

How about the typical American who drives home from a French movie in his German car, sits on *Danish* furniture in his Italian suit, drinks Brazilian coffee out of English china, listens to a Japanese *stereo*, and writes a letter on Irish *linen paper* complaining to his Congressman that too many American dollars are going *overseas*?

We really don't see ourselves, do we? We can be real *hypocrites*, complaining about problems we ourselves created.

Well, let's take a look at a less serious situation.

Do you know the difference between a French woman, an English woman, and a "blank" woman when they are kissed in bed by their husbands?

The French woman says, "Ooh, la la, Pierre, your kisses are ooh, la la."

The English woman says, "Jolly well done, Clive; I say, your kisses are jolly good."

The "blank" woman says, "You know, Frank, the ceiling needs painting."

Some people are very romantic and some obviously have other things on their minds.

And there are people who are more practical than others. Listen to this.

Three men were given only six months to live and were told they could have anything they wanted. The Frenchman wanted a *villa* on the *Riviera*. The Englishman wanted to have tea with the Queen. The "blank" man wanted the opinion of another doctor.

Now that sounds perfectly logical to me. Perhaps the "blank" man and I grew up in the same neighborhood. Well, we'll never know.

But right now what concerns me is what you know. Answer the following true-or-false questions so we can find out.

1. Christopher Columbus landed in Spain in 1492.
2. The names of some ethnic groups have been omitted from these jokes.
3. An artificial appendix is a useful organ.
4. Americans rarely buy international products.
5. All women react romantically to their husbands' kisses.

UNIT SIX, Part II

PREVIEW THESE SENTENCES
1. He *threatened* to *expose* the *traitor* and have him thrown out of their professional organization.
2. Four men *of the cloth* were having a *confidential* talk discussing their *vices*.
3. Well, how about the *hillbilly* singer who went to *Hollywood* and became a *sensation*?
4. As a country boy, he probably wasn't familiar with the tradition of *barbecuing* food on a *grill* outside, and he wasn't used to having the bathroom in the house.
5. Whether we arrived in the United States yesterday or several years ago, or are still *contemplating* our trip, we're all subject to jokes.

NOW, LET'S LAUGH
How did you do on the first part of this unit? If you're that good, you won't be confused by this next misunderstanding.

> The homeowner, Mr. Brown, asked the "blank" housepainter, Fred, what he would charge to paint his house.
> "Fifty-five dolllars a day per man—besides the paint," Fred answered.
> "You've got to be kidding," Brown said, "I wouldn't pay Rembrandt that kind of money."
> "I have news for you," said the "blank" housepainter. "If that bum charges one cent less, we'll throw him out of the *union*."

To appreciate this joke, you have to know that Rembrandt was a 17th-century *Dutch* painter. Fred, the housepainter, had clearly never heard of him. If he had, he would have known that the homeowner, Mr. Brown, was being *facetious*. Of course he wouldn't pay Rembrandt that kind of money, because Rembrandt is dead. What he meant was that he wouldn't pay any painter, even a famous one, that much money. Nevertheless, Fred took Mr. Brown's words literally and responded as any loyal union member would. He *threatened to expose the traitor* and have him thrown out of their professional organization.

Now, if you are religious, don't take this next one literally.

> Four men *of the cloth* were having a *confidential* talk discussing their *vices*. "I like *pork*," the rabbi admitted. "I drink a bottle of *scotch* a day," said the *Methodist minister*. "I have a girlfriend," *confessed* the *priest*. They all turned to the *Baptist* minister, who shrugged. "Me? I like to *gossip*."

I'm sure the leaders of your religion are above such *transgressions*, so you don't have to worry.

Consider the next jokes, about city folks and country *dwellers*. The *lifestyles* of both have their advantages and disadvantages. And you are clearly at a disadvantage when you cross over the *border*. Since I'm a city dweller, let me give you some good advice: (1) if you've never experienced life in the city, be careful and expect anything; (2) don't take everything you see and hear literally, and don't believe everything people tell you; and (3) wear your bulletproof vest, for you're bound to be the butt of somebody's humor.

Take this small-town fellow who visited New York City for the first time. He was driving his *pick-up truck*, trying to cross Fifth Avenue, and was stopped because the light was red. Then a green lit up. It read, "Walk." So he got out of his truck and walked.

Would you have done that? No, I don't think you would have, not after hearing my advice.

Well, how about the *hillbilly* singer who went to *Hollywood* and became a *sensation*? He made records, films, and a pocketful of money. He returned home one day and ran to see his father. "In California, Dad," said the hillbilly, "they do everything *backwards*. They cook in the *backyard* and have the bathroom in the house."

Why did he say that? As a country boy, he probably wasn't familiar with the tradition of *barbecuing* food on a *grill* outside, and he wasn't used to having the bathroom in the house. He and his family probably used what we call an *outhouse*.

Here's another one for you.

The traveling salesman asked a farmer, at a *rural* railroad station, why they put the *depot* so far from the town.

"I guess," the farmer answered, "they wanted it as close to the tracks as possible."

Wow! This farmer must have been joking. Surely, he knows that the railroad station and the tracks were man's creation and they were created at the same time. And what the salesman was questioning was not why the station was built so far from town, but why the tracks—the railroad itself—was built so far from town. Well, you know what I mean.

This next joke makes the city *native* look a little foolish.

A young man sitting in the subway saw an aged man smoking a cigar while sitting under a *No Smoking* sign. The young man, trying to be helpful to a stranger, said to him, "Say, Mister, you'd better stop smoking. Don't you see the sign? It says you can't smoke here."

"So what?" the elderly stranger replied. "Over there is a sign that says *Eat Cornflakes*. Does that mean I have to eat cornflakes?"

It sounds logical to me. How would you respond?

Of course, rural people like to joke about city dwellers' behavior in the country. Like the màn from Chicago who went hunting with a handful of salt, because a farmer told him the best way to catch a rabbit was to pour salt on its tail. He probably didn't get any rabbits that day—unless he could run very fast.

Well, here's one more joke that really puts the city dweller in his place.

A *Navajo Indian* came to New York City to attend college. One New Yorker noticed the Indian walking around Manhattan and asked, "How do you like our city?"

"Fine, fine," the Indian said. "And tell me: how do you like our country?"

Good for you! The Indians, the only Native Americans of America, are the *authentic* hosts of this country, and the rest of us are immigrants. So we're all in this together. Whether we arrived in the United States yesterday or several years ago, or are still *contemplating* our trip, we're all subject to jokes. Be smart: tell your jokes first about yourself and keep them laughing.

And now for a few more good laughs, answer the following true-or-false questions.

1. Rembrandt is a famous housepainter.
2. According to the joke, various religious leaders have vices.
3. If you're a stranger in the city, you shouldn't take everything you see and hear literally.
4. The best way to catch a rabbit is to put salt on its tail.
5. The authentic hosts of America are hillbillies.

UNIT SEVEN, *"Sunny California" by Art Buchwald*

PREVIEW THESE SENTENCES
1. I came to Los Angeles last week for rest and *recreation*, only to discover that it had become a *rain forest*.
2. "Why do you build your house on the top of a *canyon* when you know that during a rainstorm it has a good chance of sliding away?"
3. "Still, it must be kind of *hairy* to sit in your home during a *deluge* and wonder where you'll *wind up* next."
4. "Sure we have floods, and fire and *drought*, but that's the price you have to pay for living the good life."
5. "We would wake up in the morning and listen to the birds, and eat breakfast out on the *patio* and look down on the *smog*."

NOW, LET'S LAUGH
Here is Art Buchwald's view of life in California.

I came to Los Angeles last week for rest and *recreation*, only to discover that it had become a *rain forest*.

I didn't realize how bad it was until I went to dinner at a friend's house. I had the right address, but when I arrived, there was nothing there. I went to a neighboring house where I found a man *bailing out* his swimming pool.

"I beg your pardon," I said. "Could you tell me where the Cables live?"

"They used to live above us on the hill. Then about two years ago, their house slid down in the mud, and they lived next door to us. I think it was last Monday, during the storm, that their house slid again, and now they live two streets below us, down there. We were sorry to see them go—they were really nice neighbors."

I thanked him and slid straight down the hill to the new location of the Cables' house. Cable was clearing out mud from his car. He apologized for not giving me the new address and explained, "Frankly, I didn't know until this morning whether the house would stay here or continue sliding down a few more blocks."

"Cable," I said, "you and your wife are intelligent people. Why do you build your house on the top of a *canyon* when you know that during a rainstorm it has a good chance of sliding away?"

"We did it for the view. It really was fantastic on a clear night up there. We could sit in our *Jacuzzi* and see all of Los Angeles, except of course when there were brushfires."

"Even when our house slid down two years ago, we still had a great sight of the airport. Now I'm not sure what kind of view we'll have because of the house in front of us, which slid down with ours at the same time."

"But why don't you move to safe ground so that you don't have to worry about rainstorms?"

"We've thought about it. But once you live high in a canyon, it's hard to move to the *plains*. Besides, this house is built solid and has about three more good *mud slides* in it."

"Still, it must be kind of *hairy* to sit in your home during a *deluge* and wonder where you'll *wind up* next. Don't you ever have the desire to just *settle down* in one place?"

"It's hard for people who don't live in California to understand how we people think out here. Sure we have floods, and fire and *drought*, but that's the price you have to pay for living the good life. When Esther and I saw this house, we knew it was a dream come true. It was located right on the tippy top of the hill way up there. We would wake up in the morning and listen to the birds, and eat breakfast out on the *patio* and look down on the *smog*.

"Then after the first mud slide, we found ourselves living next to people. It was an entirely different experience. But by that time we were ready for a change. Now we've slid again, and we're in a whole new neighborhood. You can't do that if you live on solid ground. Once you move into a house below Sunset Boulevard, you're *stuck* there for the rest of your life. When you live on the side of a hill in Los Angeles, you at least know it's not going to last forever."

"Then in spite of what's happened, you don't plan to move out?"

"Are you crazy? You couldn't replace a house like this in L.A. for $500,000."

"What happens if it keeps raining and you slide down the hill again?"

"It's no problem. Esther and I figure if we slide down too far, we'll just pick up and go back to the top of the hill, and start all over again; that is, if the hill is still there after the *earthquake*."

So there's Art Buchwald's view of life in California. Let's see how well you understand it by answering the following true-or-false questions.

1. The author went to Los Angeles on business.
2. The Cables own a mobile home.
3. The Cables bought the house because of the neighbors.
4. Sunny California never has floods.
5. If the Cables' house slides too far, they'll consider moving.

UNIT EIGHT, *Health, Diet, and Exercise*

PREVIEW THESE SENTENCES
1. After a lifetime of eating the foods I enjoy, and using my *muscles* as little as possible, I have *succumbed* to *Madison Avenue's* image of the fit and attractive American, and I've changed my lifestyle.
2. My hands are faster. I can get more in my mouth before my *conscience* takes over.
3. Open mail and find final *disconnect notice* from telephone company, a threatening letter from spouse of new *flame*, and a note from a friend informing you that you have been recently *plagiarized* on *network* television.
4. People today are running, jumping, *jogging*, and *aerobic dancing*.
5. Of course, the exercise they get walking from the TV to the refrigerator is *obliterated* by the fattening *snacks* they get from the *fridge*.
6. They can't believe that with all they've done through proper diet and exercise to *circumvent* the laws of nature, they are, nevertheless, *mortal* and will eventually die.

NOW, LET'S LAUGH
Hello! Whew. You just caught me in the middle of my exercise class. After a lifetime of eating the foods I enjoy, and using my *muscles* as little as

possible, I have *succumbed* to *Madison Avenue's* image of the fit and attractive American, and I've changed my lifestyle. I am now working on a new and *trimmer* me. But it isn't easy.

The two biggest sellers in any bookstore are the cookbooks and the diet books. The cookbooks tell you how to prepare the food, and the diet books tell you how not to eat any of it.

As a result, eating isn't much fun anymore. I feel guilty whenever my fork comes near my mouth. It's gotten so bad, I've almost given up using *utensils*. My hands are faster. I can get more in my mouth before my *conscience* takes over.

Actually, the toughest part of a diet isn't watching what I eat; it's watching what my thinner friends are eating. So I tried to follow Harry Secombe's diet, which states "Eat as much as you like, just don't *swallow* it." But that's ridiculous. And frankly, so are many of the others I've heard about. There's the seafood diet—you see food and you eat it—and of course that one doesn't work. (That's a terrible pun, isn't it? You probably thought I was referring to the word **sea**, spelled s-e-a, when I was really using its *homonym*, s-e-e.)

Then there's the grapefruit diet, the Scarsdale diet, the protein diet, the carbohydrate diet, the water diet, the salt-free diet, the Pritikin Diet, the Weight Watcher's Diet, the Herbal Life Diet, the liquid diet, and the rice diet— in which you use only one *chopstick*. I quit the onion diet, 'cause while I lost ten pounds, I also lost twelve friends. It just wasn't worth it.

Johnny Carson swears he has the solution to keeping trim, with the drinking man's diet. You eat anything you want, but you must also drink two quarts of *vodka* a day. You don't lose weight; you forget you're fat. And if that doesn't work, there's always the *tranquilizer* diet. You don't lose weight, but you don't care about being fat.

People even go to diet doctors. The problem with that is that you lose more than weight. In just three weeks, my friend lost three pounds and $6,000. I have another friend who has tried everything to lose weight. Finally, she has found the formula. She eats nothing but *garlic*, onions, and *limburger cheese*. Nobody can get near her, so from a distance she looks thin.

It may not be the best solution, but it's better than what happened to a frustrated *colleague* of mine who said he'd been on a diet for two weeks and all he'd lost was two weeks. Then there's my cousin Frank, who doesn't diet at all and never gains an ounce. He eats six meals a day. An average meal consists of two steaks, four pounds of potatoes, three hamburgers, an apple pie, a milk shake, and a *hot fudge sundae*, and he still weighs the same 375 pounds.

Seriously speaking, controlling one's weight is a genuine problem that *plagues* millions of Americans, particularly those people who are concerned about their health and appearance. With my friend Susan, weighing in is actually a religious experience. When she steps on the scale and sees her weight, she usually screams, "Oh, my God! . . ." She's having trouble staying thin, or to put it another way, *battling the bulge*.

Fran Leibowitz, the well-known New York comedienne and author of two humorous books, has her own special diet plan that she logically refers to as the Fran Leibowitz High-Stress Diet. The basic diet is this: you can eat all the fattening foods you like as long as you have about an equal amount of stress and aggravation to burn up the food. For an example, listen to her mid-morning snack.

2 *glazed doughnuts*
coffee with cream and sugar
8 cigarettes
   a. Take sip of coffee.

b. Open mail and find final *disconnect notice* from telephone company, a threatening letter from spouse of new *flame*, and a note from a friend informing you that you have been recently *plagiarized* on *network* television.

Frankly, I would gladly do without the doughnuts if I could avoid those problems. Losing the use of one's telephone is bad enough in one day. But then to be threatened by the wife of the man I just started dating would just about send me running. My life is more important than cream and sugar. And then to find out that the work I had spent several years creating was now being copied on television without my being *credited* for it would just about send me over the edge. I think by the end of dinner on this kind of diet, I would have had a *stroke*. No, I don't think it's worth it. I'd be better off watching those *calories*. But thank you anyway, Ms. Leibowitz, for the thought.

Speaking of calories, what I still can't figure out is one of life's little mysteries: how can a two-pound box of candy make you gain five pounds? Do you know? Well, what difference does it make? The fact is, there are too many calories in chocolate, so I'd better stay away from it.

Calories, calories, I'm so tired of counting calories. Did you know most people can tell you more about the calories in everything they eat than how much they paid for it? Well, it's true. Listen to this.

ME: Mary, how much did your lunch cost you?
MARY: A lot. Each slice of bread was 70 calories, the pint of milk 166 calories, the *frankfurter* 248 calories, and my chocolate cake 356 calories. Can you imagine 356 calories for one piece of cake?
ME: Okay, Mary. That's enough. Thank you. Okay.

See what I mean? We are literally going crazy over calories. We're a calorie-counting culture—so much so, in fact, that some doctors think more people would stop smoking if they could prove cigarettes had calories. And that's probably true.

But calorie counting isn't enough to keep me in shape. That's why I exercise, and I'm not alone. Mary told me she had to run three miles just to work off her lunch.

Well, I don't know about you, but I'm exhausted just thinking about all that running. So, let's take a break. And while I relax, you can answer a few true-or-false questions.

1. On the Harry Secombe diet, you drink vodka all day.
2. Cigarettes have a lot of calories.
3. On the Fran Leibowitz diet, you can eat fattening foods.
4. You can lose a lot of weight on the tranquilizer diet.
5. Many people are more concerned about counting calories than the cost of their meals.

Well, that was a relaxing break. But since I still have a few minutes before I'm due back in my exercise class, I want to mention that some people exercise just to stay healthy. People today are running, jumping, *jogging*, and *aerobic dancing*. And if they don't have time to go to a class, they turn on the latest videotape of Jane Fonda, Richard Simmons, or Debbie Reynolds jumping around, and *sweat* with them.

Some of my lazier or more practical friends, however, aren't so sure this exercise business is all worth it. Patrick, a school chum of mine, said, "My doctor told me jogging could add years to my life. I think she was right. I feel ten years older already." Now, of course when Patrick's doctor said jogging would add ten years to his life, she meant that exercising would help him live ten years longer. But Patrick, tired of all the time and energy spent, interpreted his doctor's words ironically.

My neighbor, Sandy, probably agrees with him. She said, "Thanks to jogging, more people are *collapsing* in perfect health than ever before." Sounds crazy, but how else can we account for the people we read about who seemed to be in excellent physical condition and suddenly dropped dead while jogging? I don't know.

My doctor said running is healthy, and I like to think he's right. He said it's especially good for the legs, the ankles, and the economy. "The economy?" I asked. "How does it help the economy?"

"When you run," he replied, "you're helping to provide jobs for people who make sneakers, shorts, running pants, and *liniment*, and for doctors who treat people for feet and back problems and *exhaustion*."

Well, some people don't take exercise that seriously, or perhaps they have different *versions* of exercise. Joey Adams says his wife's idea of exercise is to shop faster. I can see her point. Just think of all that walking from one store to another. The faster she walks, the more calories she burns. It makes sense.

I'm not so sure about the people in *Beverly Hills*, however; you know, the ones who are considered *outdoorsmen* if they walk to their cars. They say Beverly Hills is the only place in the world where people drive three blocks to their exercise classes. Now that sounds crazy. If they're so interested in exercise, why don't they walk those three blocks? Well, some exercise is better than none.

If it weren't for the fact that the TV set and the refrigerator were so far apart, some of us wouldn't get any exercise at all. Do you know what I mean? People watching television interrupt themselves a lot to get snacks. Of course, the exercise they get walking from the TV to the refrigerator is *obliterated* by the fattening snacks they get from the *fridge*. But people aren't always rational when they're thinking about their health. You would be surprised at how much money people are willing to spend and the unpleasant things they are willing to subject themselves to, all in the name of good health and beautiful bodies.

James Coco, the late comedian and movie actor who had a weight problem most of his life, put it this way, after returning from a West Coast health spa. "Years ago, being on bread and water was a punishment. Today at a health farm, you pay a fortune for the privilege." He's right. There are people so committed to staying healthy that they are willing to pay a few hundred dollars a day at a *resort* and consume only water, grapefruit, and lettuce. At home, they might only eat foods naturally grown or those purchased in health-food stores. Staying healthy and living longer is, for them, a very serious matter.

So what happens to these people when they get sick? They are *stunned*. They feel *betrayed* by their bodies. They can't believe that with all they've done through proper diet and exercise to *circumvent* the laws of nature, they are, nevertheless, *mortal* and will eventually die. I agree with one comedian who tried to *make light* of this matter by saying, "Health nuts are going to feel stupid someday, lying in hospitals dying of nothing."

Well, since I'm not a total health nut, when I die it won't be for nothing. That is unless I'm shot for the annoying questions I ask . . . like the comprehension questions you'll find in Check Yourself, the next section in your book.

UNIT NINE, *Travel, American Style*

PREVIEW THESE SENTENCES

1. For those who are *impatient* and *artistically* undemanding, there are inexpensive *instamatics* that do just about everything automatically.

2. Usually, the only time a person looks that *ghastly* is when his or her plane is being *hijacked*.

3. There's transportation, food, *accommodations*, sightseeing tours, car rentals, *tips*, *souvenirs*, and all sorts of other trivial things to consider.

4. Then we set the lights that go on *automatically*, *activate* the *burglar alarm*, and lock all the doors and windows.

5. He should have known I was referring to the French *currency*—the *franc*—not the American food—the *frankfurter*.

6. But if you can't afford to go *abroad* this year, or on any vacation for that matter, don't *fret*; there are things you can do to give yourself and your friends the *illusion* of traveling.

NOW, LET'S LAUGH

"We are now boarding Cosmos Flight #26, *destination*: Maui, Hawaii. Will all children traveling alone, families with young children, and other passengers needing special assistance please report to gate 16 immediately. Thank you."

Okay, I'm coming. Wait for me! After all the saving, planning, and packing, I'm not going to miss my flight. But, gosh, the airport sure is crowded. It must be the season. It seems *everybody and his brother* is taking a vacation. Even the bus *terminals* and train stations are packed with tourists. How do I know they're tourists? By the cameras *dangling* from their necks and the heavy luggage dragging behind them.

Are cameras really necessary? Yes, they are, according to anybody who has ever taken a trip. Today, the question is not whether one should take a camera; the question is, what kind? For those who are impatient and *artistically* undemanding, there are inexpensive *instamatics* that do just about everything automatically. Then there are *sophisticated* models with various kinds of *lenses* that require more knowledge, interest, and work on the part of the photographer. And, of course, we have the traditional movie camera, which most people today are trading in for *video* cameras that take in the sights and sounds of everything they see.

> One friend of mine who had just returned from Paris said, "At first I thought everywhere I was going, Hollywood was making a movie, and I was in it. You can imagine my disappointment when I realized I was just surrounded by tourists taking their own home movies."

Why do tourists spend more time taking pictures than just about anything else? Joey Adams says, "The reason tourists take so many pictures is so that when they get home, they can finally see what they saw." And I think that's true. Most of us are either too cold, too hot, too tired, or too *overwhelmed* to appreciate fully the beauty in front of us. We need our cameras to help preserve our expensive and unrepeatable trips. Heaven help us, if we find out ten rolls of film later that our cameras weren't working.

And what would a trip be like without our luggage? Good question. Perhaps we should speak to a few of the many people I know who found out the answer to that question. Marilyn Tucker says she's been to Japan three times, but her luggage only once. Spencer Robbins says his luggage has traveled 20,000 miles more than he has.

If, however, you are one of the lucky ones who travel on the same plane as your luggage, let's hope you can recognize it after it's been man- and machine-handled. And don't think that if you race off the plane, and run as fast as you can to the baggage-claim area, you'll be the first to get your luggage. Whatever spot you stand in will surely be the one farthest away from where your baggage lands. Be smart, take it easy, remember that this is a vacation, and just plan to wait a long, long time. In fact, bring a snack.

In spite of the inconveniences, however, vacations are necessary. You need to get away from your daily routine. How do you know you're ready for one?

Just look at your passport. If you start to look like your picture, you know you need it bad. Usually, the only time a person looks that *ghastly* is when his or her plane is being *hijacked*.

Now that you have established the fact that you need it, where do you go? And if you're married, should you or your spouse decide? My brother's wife has a good system. Each year she says, "We'll go anywhere you want." Then she hands my brother a list of the places she likes.

But the problem with most vacations is that we sometimes expect too much. A vacation is a holiday away from everything except expenses. And there's no getting away from them. There's transportation, food, *accommodations*, sightseeing tours, car rentals, *tips*, *souvenirs*, and all sorts of other trivial things to consider. So plan ahead, and start saving. Listen to this couple, and see how they're doing.

> "Good news, Bob! I've saved enough money for us to go to Europe."
> "Wonderful," he said. "When do we leave, Jane?"
> "As soon as I've saved enough for us to come back."

Keep saving. Better yet, Jane, read one of those books on the market that tell you how to travel economically. The question is, do they help? My neighbor Alex told me, "We just got back in town, and you know that book that tells you how to have a wonderful vacation for $10 a day? Well, now I know how to do it. You stay home and read that book!"

Now wait a minute. Things can't be that bad. My neighbor probably didn't follow the instructions. If you have to watch your pennies, you just don't travel first class. One comedian said, "In America, there are two classes of travel—first class and with your children." That's for sure.

But when we speak about another class of travel, we're really talking about tourist class, or economy, and if you travel that way, you are bound to save some money. By planning and preparing *thoroughly*, you can have fun as well. But you can't leave everything to the last minute. Listen to my friends Nina and Cliff.

> Whenever we start a vacation, it's the same thing. We get up at six o'clock in the morning to get an early start. First we eat breakfast; then we pack; then we *notify* the neighbors and police department; then we stop the milk, mail, and newspaper deliveries; then we arrange for a kid to *mow* the *lawn* and water the garden; then we take the dog to the *kennel*; then the kids say goodbye to their friends; then we set the lights that go on *automatically*, *activate* the *burglar alarm*, and lock all the doors and windows. After all this is finally done, you know what we do? We go to bed, because I hate night driving!

You waited too long to get ready, Cliff, and maybe you should have taken a plane. Well, now, before we wait too long, let's take a break so you can review what you've heard.

Back already? You must have taken a plane! You know, many people prefer to fly, because it doesn't matter what time of day they want to leave. And they can go just about anywhere. While I'm flying to Hawaii, thousands of other Americans are flying to foreign lands. Americans love to go *abroad*.

The big problem is that not many of us are good at foreign languages. In fact, if you've ever seen us attempting to speak French or Italian or Chinese, you would never be embarrassed about your own mistakes in English. We really envy those who can speak other languages. Mark Twain, the 19th-century humorist, said he was particularly impressed with the children of Paris—because even the five-year-olds could speak French!

> Then there's my friend, Luke. When I asked him, "Did you have any trouble with your French when you were abroad?" he said, "No, but the French did."

After talking further to Luke, I can see why the French had difficulty understanding him. When I asked, "Did you get any French *francs*?" he said, "Yeah, but they're not as good as our hot dogs." See what I mean? He should have known I was referring to the French *currency*—the franc—not the American food—the *frankfurter*. Well, I'm not surprised he was confused, considering the kinds of French lessons he took. He said he learned French in six easy "*liaisons*." Obviously, they weren't enough. And they were "liaisons"—that is, love affairs—not structured language "lessons."

On the other hand, some Americans think they can speak English anywhere. James Thurber, another humorist, tells the story of a famous editor trying to get around Paris. This editor thought that, if the French didn't understand him, it was only because they couldn't hear him. So he talked louder and louder until he ended up *SHOUTING* at them.

We've probably all made mistakes that are equally laughable. That's part of the fun of traveling abroad. But if you can't afford to go *abroad* this year, or on any vacation for that matter, don't *fret*; there are things you can do to give yourself and your friends the *illusion* of traveling. For example:

> If you don't go on a vacation this year, you can get the feel of one by tipping every third person you see.

Do you understand the joke? Tipping is so much a part of any vacation that tipping people you see throughout the day should help you feel as though you are traveling.

If you don't like that ridiculous idea, do what my cousin Diana did to fool your friends. She signed up for one of those economy *cruises* but stayed home and had the company send her picture postcards so she could mail them out from her home at the appropriate times.

These *tactics* don't really help, I suppose. If you really want to travel but can't afford it, the only thing I can say to *console* you is, consider the advantages of staying home. Think of my friend Lilly, who went on a vacation she'll never forget. Why? Because the *charge slips* keep reminding her. What a *burden*! Consider all that money she's spending now that she's back at work, paying for a vacation that is just a memory.

Still, here I am, about to board a plane for Hawaii, and happy as can be. I'm even singing a little song to myself.

> As for me, I'd even climb a tree to be free.
> I don't need to look at my passport to know—I need it bad, my *morale* is low.
> So, if you'll excuse me, my plane awaits. I'd ask you some questions, but I can't be late.
> All I can do is offer suggestions—make up your own true-or-false questions.
> Don't worry; I'll see you again. But right now, it's *Aloha*, my friends.

UNIT TEN, *All Our Funny Friends*

PREVIEW THESE SENTENCES

1. The best laughs of all were had at The Friars, a world-famous theatrical club in New York City where Joey Adams invited us to attend a special *testimonial* dinner called a "roast."

2. And after we've all laughed ourselves sick over the insults directed at the guest of honor, the *honoree* then has an opportunity to *retaliate* and respond to all that's been said.

3. "We really love each other—and if you believe that, I have some *swampland* in Jersey I'd like to *unload* on you."

4. "*Misers* aren't fun to live with, but they make wonderful *ancestors*."

5. "My parents didn't want me—they put a live *teddy bear* in my *crib*."

6. "You can always tell a *widow* in Beverly Hills. She wears a black *tennis outfit*."

NOW, LET'S LAUGH

I'm back from *paradise*, and what a great time I had. Not only did I visit Hawaii, but on my way home, I stopped off in Hollywood, California, and New York City, the two *show-business* capitals of the world. And who should I run into but many of our famous funny friends, past and present.

In Hollywood I had a chance to visit the exciting movie and *television studios* where comedians like the following performed their magic: Eddie Cantor, Jack Benny, Bob Hope, Edgar Bergen, George Burns and Gracie Allen, Lucille Ball and Desi Arnaz, and Groucho Marx and his brothers. Then I saw Dean Martin and Jerry Lewis, Laurel and Hardy, Abbott and Costello, Jackie Gleason and Art Carney, Peter Sellers, Danny Kaye, Sid Caesar and Imogene Coca, the Smothers Brothers, Carol Burnett and Harvey Korman, Lily Tomlin, Joan Rivers, Jonathan Winters, Bob Newhart, John Ritter, Bill Cosby, and Woody Allen—just to mention a few.

When I had to leave these terrific *personalities*, I didn't feel too bad, because I knew that I would meet many more in New York. In the nightclubs and in the Catskill Mountains, a resort area near New York City, I was certain to hear Don Rickles, Richard Pryor, Mort Sahl, Lenny Bruce, Dick Gregory, David Frye, Mike Nichols, and Elaine May. Also, I heard George Carlin, Alan King, Dom Deluise, Eddie Murphy, Buddy Hackett, Billy Crystal, and the list goes on.

The best laughs of all were had at The Friars, a world-famous theatrical club in New York City where Joey Adams invited us to attend a special *testimonial* dinner called a "roast." What's a roast? It's a *fund-raising* activity that honors a celebrity in a unique way—by making fun of him or her. And the Friars, which is internationally known for its annual roast of entertainers, raises money for needy show-business people and for other *worthy causes*. At these dinners, attended by more than a thousand guests, there are several carefully selected people sitting on the *dais* who provide entertainment by speaking for about five minutes in a negatively humorous way. And after we've all laughed ourselves sick over the insults directed at the guest of honor, the *honoree* then has an opportunity to *retaliate* and respond to all that's been said.

How did such a club and such an activity get started? It was founded in 1907 by *press agents* who were always looking for ways to *promote* their clients. Since this idea of giving dinners to noted *producers*, theater owners, and actors successfully attracted publicity, the tradition continues today.

> Johnny Carson says, "We only roast those we love. Everything we say here tonight is strictly for laughs. We really love each other—and if you believe that, I have some *swampland* in Jersey I'd like to *unload* on you.

What can you do with these comedians? Even when Johnny Carson seemed to be saying something nice and *sentimental*, he really meant it ironically. The joke here is this: if you are *gullible* enough to buy swampland that is totally useless, you'll "buy"—that is, you'll believe—anything you hear. But not you! By now, you have developed an ear for jokes, and you won't be anyone's victim any more, though that's not so bad when you consider the long, impressive list of people—many funny comedians—who have been the butt of Friars' jokes.

For our final visit together, let's sit back and enjoy the jokes of some of Joey Adams' funny friends, many of them Friars. And this time, we will limit the explanations. Why ruin your fun? We'll let you and your partner try to figure them out.

> And now, ladies and gentlemen, let me introduce you to one of America's first television comedians, Milton Berle, who became a comedian when

his mother gave him a mouthful of marbles. He dropped the marbles out of his mouth one by one, and when they discovered what he'd done, they said he'd *lost all of his marbles.*

Steve Martin's father gave him a rocking chair. He rocked on it day and night until one day it broke, and then they discovered he was *off his rocker.*

Don Adams: "I'm sure my wife will live forever. She has nothing but dresses she *wouldn't be found dead in.*"

Rodney Dangerfield always begins with his *trademark* line: "I get no respect. The way my luck is running, if I were a politician, I'd be honest."

How's your luck running? Do you understand what you've heard? Check by answering these true-or-false questions.

1. Hawaii is the show-business capital of the world.
2. The Catskill Mountains is a resort area near New York City.
3. Only people who are hated are roasted.
4. Milton Berle became a comedian when his mother bought him a rocking chair.
5. The swampland that Johnny Carson talked about is valuable land in New Jersey.

Now let's visit a few more of Joey Adams' funny friends.

David Brenner: "*Misers* aren't fun to live with, but they make wonderful *ancestors.*"

George Carlin points out that the value of the dollar is decreasing, while the price of bread is going up—"The *moral* is: save bread."

Woody Allen, comedian, actor, writer, director, and producer, says: "My parents didn't want me—they put a live *teddy bear* in my crib."

Robert Klein: "It's really not the doctor or nurses or hospitals that are the problem. It's the side effects—like bankruptcy."

David Steinberg: "Insanity is grounds for divorce in some states, but grounds for marriage in all; marriage is like a *cafeteria*—you pick out something good-looking and pay later.

David Letterman: "A woman's place is in the home, and she should go there directly from work."

Danny Thomas got a letter he couldn't read. "It's either from my four-year-old-grandson," he said, "or my 40-year-old-doctor."

Joan Rivers: "You can always tell a *widow* in Beverly Hills. She wears a black *tennis outfit.*"

Groucho Marx said after reviewing the performance of a play titled *Dreadful Night*: "I saw the show at a disadvantage—the *curtain* was up."

Don Rickles: "I love Joey Adams' humor. I have no taste, but I love him."

Lily Tomlin, playing a telephone operator, says to a customer, "Wouldn't you rather pay than lose your service, and possibly an eye?"

When Bob Hope received a *plaque* from the Friars, he *modestly* said, "I don't really deserve this honor, but on the other hand I've got *arthritis* and I don't deserve that either."

Phyllis Diller's advice to brides: "Burn the toast so he won't notice the coffee."

Bill Dana on the high cost ($18,000) of an *astronaut's* space suit: "But it has two pairs of pants."

Bob Hope: "You know you're getting older when it takes you longer to rest than to get tired."

Billy Crystal complains about the poor performance of the Chicago Cubs baseball team: "The *fans* are beginning to order *take-out* food."

Joan Rivers notes, "For fixing things around the house, nothing beats a man who's *handy* with a *checkbook.*"

Dom Deluise: "Adam may have had his troubles, but he never had to listen to Eve talk about the other men she could have married."

Bill Cosby even makes jokes about English: "If you go to New England, a man can die of a hat attack." (He says this because New Englanders pronounce "heart" almost like "hat.")

Finally, Carl Reiner: "The guy was up all night and looked like a mess. He explained to his pal, 'I haven't been home all night because I'm afraid of my wife. She knew I had $500 in my pocket last night and she knew I was going to play poker, but she thought it was a 10-cent game. Well, I lost every cent—all $500—and I can't face her.' His friend felt sorry for him and lent him the $500 and told him to go home and face his wife. He said, 'Thanks, pal. Can you do me one more favor? Can you let me have another $100? I'd like to show her I was a winner.'"

Speaking of winners, a comedian isn't a winner every night, no matter how talented or famous he or she is. Either his timing is off, her material is inappropriate for the audience that *drifted in*, he doesn't feel well, she just got some bad news right before she stepped on stage, or he just isn't in the mood to be funny. What then? When the experienced performer notices he is losing his audience—by the talking, the lack of laughter, and perhaps the parade of people heading for the door—he will pull out of his memory what those in the trade call "savers." Even Lucille Ball, Bob Hope, George Burns, and Johnny Carson have their share of those *life preservers*—lines that can turn a hostile audience into *responsive* fans.

Milton Berle said one time when things weren't going well, "Ever get the feeling you're in the wrong business?" Henny Youngman *defused* his bombs with, "I want to thank you for coming to my *funeral*." And Bob Hope turned on the laughter with: "Please come back to see me again, but not as a group."

Finally, our lifesaver is: We enjoyed your company. You've been a patient and hardworking audience. We hope, for your sake, that you find something to laugh at every day. Because, as many people have discovered, you will probably "live longer through laughter," or at least more happily, and that's what we want for you. And that's no joke!

One last time, then, check yourself by answering the comprehension questions in your book.

Answer Key

Introduction, Part I

NOW, LET'S LAUGH
1. False (he hated the book; he enjoyed the movie)
2. False (unexpected and illogical)
3. True

COMPREHENSION CHECK
1. Americans treat their pets like friends, and Americans compare the movies they see with the books on which these movies were based.
2. One must be familiar with what is normal and usual behavior in order to recognize an exaggerated, twisted, or altered point of view.
3. A sudden alteration of point of view is the main ingredient.

Introduction, Part II

NOW, LET'S LAUGH
1. True
2. False (it is a put-down joke)
3. False (they often use stereotypes)

COMPREHENSION CHECK
1. They both have unexpected endings. The put-down joke is insulting.
2. The word *herd* is used to mean a bunch of cows, and the word *heard* is used as the past tense of the word *hear*.
3. Stereotyped Texans are very rich and big spenders.

Unit One, Part I

NOW, LET'S LAUGH
1. False (many ways)
2. True

3. False (not successful; *to bomb* means "to fail")
4. True

COMPREHENSION CHECK
1. The tone of voice, the stress, and the pacing contribute to the delivery.
2. He can deliver it with a certain inflection, use an accent, "throw it away," or be sarcastic.
3. It gives the audience a chance to digest all the information they've heard, and it creates suspense as it signals that the climax is about to come.
4. He was amazed that he was alive, because his wife was driving much too fast and she was a "new" driver.

Unit One, Part II

NOW, LET'S LAUGH
1. False (he lost his money because his horse lost the race)
2. True
3. False (Becky didn't even know about John Glenn or his achievement)
4. False (Fox didn't want to go to work)

COMPREHENSION CHECK
1. Pacing is the speed at which one speaks and the length and frequency of pauses separating units of thought.
2. He didn't want to go to work.
3. Affectionate words like *hugging* and *kissing* were used to describe what the horse and jockey were doing.
4. It is an anticlimax joke.
5. Jones was afraid he would die.

Unit Two, Part I

NOW, LET'S LAUGH
1. False (people often joke about their work)
2. True
3. False (he thought it was appendicitis)
4. True
5. False (the greed of lawyers)

COMPREHENSION CHECK
1. The joke about the lawyer and the hostile witness is an example of a put-down joke.
2. The patient died.
3. He told the doctor to do what most doctors tell their patients.
4. They respond with routine advice: take two aspirins and call back later.

Unit Two, Part II

NOW, LET'S LAUGH
1. c   2. b   3. d   4. a

COMPREHENSION CHECK
1. He takes his orders too literally, and he doesn't know much about food preparation.
2. He taught his wife to swim.
3. He felt the actor was not very good and would be a better butcher than an actor.
4. He had to give up his expensive store because business was bad.

Unit Three, Part I

NOW, LET'S LAUGH
1. True
2. False (more likely to listen to humorous criticism)
3. True
4. False (he even tells jokes about his age)
5. False (the U.N. was constructed on land Mr. Rockefeller's father donated)

COMPREHENSION CHECK
1. They joke about them to make a political point that people might not listen to if it were delivered in a serious manner and because they are in the news.
2. Newsmakers like the President, congressmen, and various government bureaucrats are regular butts on his show.
3. He felt he would win more support by responding humorously and showing off his keen wit and his ability to handle situations than by seriously answering every question reporters asked.
4. They represent the people of the U.S., and they are accountable to them. Therefore, what they do and don't do is important to the people who vote for them.
5. He wanted to turn it into a joke.

Unit Three, Part II

NOW LET'S LAUGH
1. False (several write books and television scripts and give lectures)
2. True
3. True
4. True

COMPREHENSION CHECK
1. It is an example of an anticlimax joke.
2. They have to make many promises to many people.
3. She will never admit that she is as old as 35, the required age.
4. Politicians are responsible for creating very complicated situations.

Unit Four, Part I

NOW, LET'S LAUGH
1. False (they tell secrets)
2. True
3. False (children tell Santa what they want)
4. True
5. True

COMPREHENSION CHECK
1. They say anything that pops into their minds and tell their parents' secrets.
2. His book tells him how well or badly children have behaved during the year.

3. They tell them that storks deliver babies.

4. She knows that it isn't normal for a child to arrive by a stork.

5. They question their parents' authority, rebel at society's rules, and don't help around the house.

Unit Four, Part II

NOW LET'S LAUGH

1. True
2. False (some mothers want more for their daughters)
3. False (mothers are like chauffeurs driving their children different places)
4. False (not as badly)
5. False (omitted from wills)

COMPREHENSION CHECK

1. He talks about her.
2. They want to know how she and her husband will live, what kind of husband their son-in-law will be, and whether he will earn a good income.
3. Mothers don't always want the same things for their daughters and their daughters-in-law. In the joke, it was fine for the daughter to have a maid and do little work around the house, but it was not fine for the son's wife to have a maid and do little work around the house.
4. Fathers appear to misunderstand their children and make a terrible mess when they do something around the house.
5. He expected to find out that his uncle had left him money and other valuables.

Unit Five, Part I

NOW, LET'S LAUGH

1. True
2. True
3. False (it encourages them to marry)
4. False (some happily married people tell such jokes)
5. False (the wife is in charge in many homes)

COMPREHENSION CHECK

1. Both may have frantic activity.

2. The speaker smiles or speaks in a playful or sarcastic tone of voice. The speaker may begin a joke in very general terms, or the speaker may talk about people you don't know.

3. They aren't happy, or they think society expects them to joke about marriage, or they are superstitious.

4. They don't fight because the wife makes all the important decisions.

5. He wanted her to admit that he was right.

Unit Five, Part II

NOW LET'S LAUGH

1. True
2. True
3. False (according to the Bible, Eve was created from Adam's rib)
4. False (the number of divorces has nothing to do with the size and weight of a wedding ring)
5. False (in case there is a divorce)

COMPREHENSION CHECK

1. One cause is cheating.
2. She wanted to see if Adam was seeing another woman.
3. She learned he was cheating.
4. They sign them to avoid disagreements regarding how the couple's estate will be divided up in the event of a divorce.
5. Divorce is so prevalent.

Unit Six, Part I

NOW, LET'S LAUGH

1. False (Columbus landed in America in 1492)
2. True
3. False (even a real appendix is useless)
4. False (Americans buy many products from abroad)
5. False (some women don't)

COMPREHENSION CHECK

1. They turn away or leave the room.
2. It is illogical that the man would throw away his peanut butter sandwich, because he made it himself.

159

3. This American is a hypocrite because he says one thing (keep dollars in the United States) and does another (buys goods from other countries).

4. The Frenchman wanted a villa on the Riviera, the Englishman wanted tea with the Queen, but the "blank," who was the most practical, wanted another doctor's opinion.

Unit Six, Part II

NOW LET'S LAUGH

1. False (Rembrandt [1606–69] was a great Dutch artist)
2. True
3. True
4. False (a rabbit won't let you get close enough to put salt on its tail)
5. False (the American Indians)

COMPREHENSION CHECK

1. Fred wanted to punish any painter who would work for less. Apparently, he didn't know that Rembrandt was a famous artist who lived 300 years ago.
2. He drank a bottle of scotch (whiskey) every day.
3. The "walk" sign is only for pedestrians—that is, people who are walking—and not for people driving trucks and cars.
4. Californians cooked in the backyard and had their bathroom in the house; where he came from, it was just the opposite.
5. The Navajos and other Indians lived in the United States before any other group, but today, ironically, they are treated like outsiders.

Unit Seven

NOW, LET'S LAUGH

1. False (he went for rest and recreation)
2. True (the term *mobile home*, however, usually refers to a trailer, or a home on wheels, which can be pulled by a car)
3. False (they bought it for the view)
4. False (California often has floods)
5. True

COMPREHENSION CHECK

1. The Cables' house kept sliding because of the mud on the mountain.
2. They benefitted because, each time they slid, they had new neighbors and new experiences.
3. Cable said the house was worth $500,000. It has a Jacuzzi and a patio, and a neighboring house has a swimming pool.
4. Los Angeles homeowners have problems with floods, fire, drought, earthquakes, and mudslides.
5. The Cables are willing to start all over, at the top of the hill.

Unit Eight

NOW LET'S LAUGH

1. False (the Secombe diet requires you to eat without swallowing)
2. False (if they did, more people would quit smoking)
3. True
4. False (but you don't care about being fat)
5. True

COMPREHENSION CHECK

1. The two best-sellers are cookbooks and diet books. The first tells you how to eat well, but the second tells you how to stop eating well.
2. The Harry Secombe diet tells you to eat without swallowing, but then you're not eating. The rice diet asks you to eat with only one chopstick, but you can't get any food unless you have two chopsticks. The onion diet makes your breath bad, so you lose friends; the same is true of diets of limburger cheese and garlic. Johnny Carson's vodka diet doesn't make you lose weight; it only makes you drunk. And the tranquilizer diet only makes you stop caring.
3. The speaker would rather be fat than have Ms. Leibowitz's stress.
4. The speaker is tired of counting calories, and her friend Mary tells what a meal "cost" in calories rather than in dollars and cents.
5. Jogging requires special clothes, medicines, and sometimes a doctor's treatment.

6. People who take good care of their bodies feel betrayed when they get sick.

7. The speaker says "it isn't easy," "eating is not much fun any more," she "feels guilty," she doesn't like watching what her thinner friends are eating, that "controlling one's weight is a genuine problem that plagues millions of Americans," and that she's "tired of counting calories."

Unit Nine

COMPREHENSION CHECK

1. The first people to board are children traveling alone, families with small children, and people who need special assistance.

2. We recognize tourists by their cameras and heavy luggage.

3. An instamatic camera requires no patience.

4. According to Joey Adams, it's to see what they saw.

5. Tourist problems are climate changes, fatigue, lost luggage, and lots of expenses.

6. Alex felt that the book didn't work: "Well, now I know how you do it. You stay home and read that book!"

7. Even the five-year-olds could speak French!

8. Luke's French was so bad that he thought "francs" were frankfurters.

He studied French only in liaisons and not in lessons.

9. You can tip every third person or have someone else send postcards in your name.

10. The main advantage of staying home is that you save money.

Unit Ten

NOW, LET'S LAUGH

1. False (Hawaii is a vacation center)

2. True

3. False (comedians often roast people they like and admire)

4. False (when she gave him a mouthful of marbles)

5. False (swampland usually has little value)

COMPREHENSION CHECK

1. A "roast" is a fund-raising activity in which comedians make jokes about a celebrity.

2. The Friars were founded in 1907 by press agents trying to get more publicity for the comedians they represented.

3. Since "losing your marbles" has two meanings, it's a wordplay.

4. "I get no respect."

5. They put a live teddy bear in his crib.

6. Bad news, bad timing, illness, and the wrong mood can all cause comedians to perform badly.

Glossary

abroad (adv.): out of the country

absurd (adj.): foolish, silly

abuse (v.): treat badly; misuse

accommodations (n.): places to stay, such as hotels

accusation (n.): a charge, or statement, of wrongdoing

acrobat (n.): person with excellent body control who does gymnastic feats (e.g., in a circus)

adopt (v.): take as one's own, as in "adopt a child" or "adopt an idea"

advent (n.): a beginning, a coming, or an arrival

advertise (v.): give public notice of; announce

aerobic dancing (n.): exercises in the form of dancing

affectionate (adj.): loving

agency (n.): a place of business that acts for someone or something

alimony (n.): regular payments to a former spouse

alteration (n.): a change

amazed (adj.): filled with wonder; very surprised

ancestor (n.): a family member—such as great-grandparents—from whom we came

angel (n.): an unusually good person; like the spirits in Heaven

anonymous (adj.): by a person whose name is unknown

apologize (v.): say one is sorry

appendix (n.); appendicitis (n.): a useless organ in the body; the illness it causes

appoint (v.): assign or name to a position

arthritis (n.): a painful disease of the joints (where the bones meet)

artificial (adj.): not natural or real

aspirin (n.): a medicine for headaches

assault (n.): an attack

astonished (adj.): very surprised; amazed

astronaut (n.): a traveler in outer space

attentive (adj.): caring, thoughtful, watchful

auditorium (n.): a large space in a building for public events

authentic (adj.): real, true

backyard (n.): a grassy area behind a house

Baptist minister (n.): a leader of a Protestant (Christian) religious group

bequest (n.): a gift left by a dead person to a friend or relative

Beverly Hills (n.): a wealthy town where many movie stars live and shop

BMW (n.): a high-priced German automobile

boast (v.): speak too highly of oneself

border (n.): outer part encircling something (e.g., around a picture); or as a boundary (e.g., separating two countries)

bowling alley (n.): an indoor place where a game called *bowling* is played

bum (n.): a person who moves around, doesn't work, and appears to be lazy

bunch (n.): a group of things of the same kind

burden (n.): a heavy responsibility or load

bureaucrat (n.): a person who works in a government office

burglar alarm (n.): a device that alerts one to the presence of an intruder

butt of a joke (n.): an object of humor; a person or thing being made fun of

Cadillac (n.): a high-priced American car

cafeteria (n.): an eating place where people serve themselves

calculating (adj.): scheming; always trying to win

calories (n.): units of energy given to the body by food

campaign (n.): a series of activities necessary to win a political office

canyon (n.): low-lying land between two mountains or cliffs

catalyst (n.): something/someone that causes change in something/someone (usually a chemical term)

charge (v.): ask for payment

chauffeur (v.): drive another person from place to place

cheap person (n.): one who holds tightly to money, who doesn't like to spend money

checkbook (n.): a book containing checks—forms to make payments from money in one's own bank

chopstick (n.): one of two sticks used by Orientals for picking up food

chore (n.): a duty; a task

cleanliness (n.): cleanness

client (n.): a customer, in certain professions (e.g., lawyers, accountants)

clue (n.): an idea or information leading to the solution of a problem

clue in (v.): make one aware; help one understand something

colleague (n.): associate; fellow worker

comedian (n.): a person who tells jokes; a funny person

communicator (n.): a person who is good with words

complaint (n.): finding fault

compliment (v.): say kind words about someone else

comprise (v.): contain, include

confidential (adj.): spoken or written as a secret

constitute (v.): make up, add up to

convenient (adj.): suited to personal comfort or easy performance

cool down (v.): to become calmer; to lose ardor or passion

cosmetic/plastic surgeon (n.): a doctor who improves one's appearance through operations

crib (n.): a bed for a baby

criticize (v.); criticism (n.): judge or say unkind things; an unkind statement or judgment

cruise (n.): a vacation trip on a large boat

curtain (n.): a hanging screen usually capable of being drawn back or up

cynic (n.): a person who doubts or disbelieves

dais (n.): a raised part of the floor, for speakers to stand on

dangling (adj.): hanging loosely; not secure

Danish (adj.): referring to the people of Denmark

day camp (n.): a place that offers daytime entertainment for children on summer vacation

decent (adj.): well-behaved; free of bad qualities

despair (v.): give up hope; become very unhappy

destination (n.): a place that is to be the end of a journey

diet (n.): food and drink to improve health and appearance

digest (v.): think about or arrange

disgust (n.): a dislike; an extremely negative feeling

disharmony (n.): a lack of peacefulness or order

docile (adj.): easily taught; obedient

donate (v.): give

drought (n.): a long period of dry weather

drowsily (adj.): sleepily; without being awake

drunk (n.): a person who drinks too much alcohol

dual (adj.): double

Dutch (adj.): referring to the people of Holland

dweller (n.): one who lives inside something, such as a city-dweller

earth at my feet (idiom): to have everything one wants, as in "Winning the election put the earth at my feet."

earthquake (n.): a shaking of the ground

emphasis (n.): stress; forceful expression

entertainer (n.): one who performs professionally for an audience, such as a singer or a comedian

entitle (v.): give the right to do something

erector set (n.): a children's box of sticks and braces for building structures

estate (n.): all of a person's goods, money, and property

exaggerate (v.): to go beyond the truth in something

explorer (n.): a person who travels to unknown lands

extramarital affair (n.): a sexual friendship with a person who is not one's husband or wife

fairy tale (n.): a simple story for children, full of unreal events

fan (n.): an enthusiastic supporter of a sports team, type of music, etc.

favorite (adj.): best-liked

fiancé (n.): a man (**fiancée:** a woman) who is engaged to be married

fire (v.): dismiss from a job; terminate a person's employment

forbidden (adj.): not allowed; not permitted

franc (n.): the French unit of currency

frankfurter (n.): a traditional American sausage (meat), hot dog

frantic (adj.): almost out of control; highly nervous

fret (v.): worry, trouble one's self

funeral (n.): a ceremony honoring a dead person

fur (n.): an animal's coat used to make clothing

gambling (n.): playing games, such as card games, to win money

garlic (n.): a spice with a strong odor and taste

genius (n.): a person with unusual intelligence or creative ability

genuine (adj.): real, true

ghastly (adj.): frightening; very unpleasant

glazed doughnut (n.): a sugar-coated pastry with a hole in the middle

godliness (n.): the state of being like God, or living as God wishes

gossip (v.): repeat what one knows about other people

greed (n.): a very strong desire for food or money

grief (n.): deep sadness; emotional suffering

grill (v.): cook on a metal rack over a flame

grounds (for divorce) (n.): reason (for ending marriage)

herd (n.): a number of animals, such as cows or sheep, kept together

hint (n.): a suggestion given indirectly

hire (v.): employ for wages; give a job to

holler (v.): shout, cry out, yell

Hollywood (n.): the Los Angeles district where films are made

homonym (n.): a word that sounds exactly like another word but has a different meaning

honoree (n.): a person who receives an honor

hot fudge sundae (n.): a dessert made with ice cream and chocolate

hover (v.): hang over or about; stay near

illusion (n.): an appearance which is not real

image (n.): a mental picture; a form, outline, or appearance

immigrant (n.): a person who comes into a foreign country to live

impressionist (n.): one who imitates others

in advance (adj.): prior, before

incompetent (adj.): without ability or qualifications

indescribable (adj.): beyond words; impossible to explain

indifference (n.): lack of feeling or opinion

indignant (adj.): feeling offended

ingredient (n.): one item in a mixture; in cooking, each of the items put into a food

initially (adv.): at the beginning

inmate (n.): a person kept in a prison, hospital, etc.

instamatic (n.): a small, easy-to-use camera

interpret (v.): to give one's explanation of something (e.g., an event, fact)

ironic (adj.): expressing the opposite of what is really meant

Jacuzzi (n.): a hot bath or pool for relaxation

jogging (n.): running slowly, usually for exercise

judge (v.): form or state an opinion

jury (n.): a group of people who make a decision in a law case

keen (adj.): sharp, pointed

kennel (n.): a house for dogs

kidnap (v.): carry a person away and hold the person

lawn (n.): a neat area of grass, usually around a house

lens (n.): the glass in a camera, microscope, etc.

lifestyle (n.): the way one lives

limburger cheese (n.): a soft, strong-smelling cheese

linen paper (n.): fine writing paper

liniment (n.): a liquid treatment for the skin

lonesome (adj.): lonely; alone

look up (v.): find the source; search for

lousy (adj.): bad, unpleasant, poor

Madison Avenue (n.): a street in New York full of advertising agencies

maid (n.): a woman who cleans rooms, washes dishes, etc.

malicious (adj.): evil, vicious

marble (n.): a small glass ball for children's play

mechanics (n.): working structure; procedure

merchandise (n.): goods to buy or sell

message (n.): a written or oral communication

Methodist minister (n.): a leader of a Protestant (Christian) religious group

millionaire (n.): a person who is worth $1 million or more

minimize (v.): make or keep small

minorities (n.): Americans who are either not white or not Christian

miser (n.): a person who lives poorly in order to get rich

misfortune (n.): bad luck

mobile (adj.): movable or capable of moving

monologue (n.): a long speech by one person; a soliloquy

moral (n.): a lesson; the practical message of a story

mortal (adj.): living and capable of dying

movie (n.): a moving picture; a film

mow (v.): cut grass, cut down

mundane (adj.): ordinary

muscles (n.): the parts of the body that cause movement

mutter (v.): speak softly or badly such that others cannot understand

nap (n.): a short sleep, usually during the day

native (n.): a person who has lived in a certain place a very long time

Navajo Indian (n.): an American Indian living in the Southwest of the United States

ne'er-do-well (adj.): never succeeding; always doing badly

network television (n.): programs shown across the country by a company owning many stations

newspaper column (n.): a regular article written by the same person

night court (n.): a place where justice is administered after normal working hours

nonchalant (adj.): carefree, relaxed

notify (v.): to report the occurrence of a situation

nudge (v.): push gently; send a signal by touch

obedience (n.): following direction; respecting authority

obviously (adv.): clearly; unmistakably

old-timer (n.): a person who has been around a long time; an older person

optometrist (n.): a doctor who examines and measures eyes

outdoorsman (n.): person who prefers to spend a lot of time outside

overseas (adv.): across the sea; abroad

oversimplified (adj.): expressed so simply that the true meaning is changed or lost

painstakingly (adv.): very carefully and completely

paradise (n.): Heaven; a place of perfect happiness; in the Bible, the Garden of Eden, home of Adam and Eve

patience (n.): the ability to wait for something calmly, for a long time

patio (n.): a space with a stone floor, outside a house, for relaxing

pay back (v.): give the same treatment as received

pay over (v.): make a formal payment of

peals (of laughter) (n.): loud, long laughter, or a number of laughs one after another

peanut butter sandwich (n.): two slices (or a slice) of bread covered with a filling like butter, but which tastes like peanuts

personalities (n.): people well known to the public

physician (n.): a doctor; someone who treats diseases with medicine

pickup truck (n.): a light truck with an open body usually used to transport large objects

plague (v.): annoy, bother

plaque (n.): a flat wood or metal plate, usually with writing on it, fixed to a wall in memory of a person or event

plumber (n.): a person whose job is to fit and repair water pipes

plump (adj.): nicely rounded; rather fat; well covered with flesh

poke fun at (idiom): to make jokes against

Pop (n.): Dad; Father

pop (v.): come or enter suddenly, unexpectedly

pork (n.): the meat from pigs

portion (n.): a part separated or cut off; a share of something that is divided among two or more people

possessive (adj.): unwilling to share one's own things with other people; wanting the full attention of someone else

pout (v.): show childish bad temper and displeasure

prank (n.): a playful but foolish trick, not intended to harm

precede (v.): go in front of

prenuptial (adj.): before marriage

preoccupation (n.): the state known as "lost in thought;" giving full attention to something

pressure (n.): trouble that causes anxiety and difficulty; strong influence

prevalent (adj.): existing commonly, generally, or widely in some place or time

priest (n.): a man in a Christian church trained for religious duties (e.g., performing ceremonies and services)

psychiatrist (n.): a doctor who treats diseases of the mind

publicity (n.): public notice or attention

pump (v.): move up and down; force something steadily into or out of

punch line (n.): the last few words of a joke or story that give meaning to the whole and cause amusement or surprise

rabbi (n.): a leader in the Jewish religion

rage (n.): a sudden feeling of uncontrollable anger

rain forest (n.): a wet tropical forest with tall trees growing thickly together

realtor (n.): a person who sells property (land, homes, apartments)

recall (v.): remember

reflect (v.): to think back on or to think over something in the past; to show an image (e.g., as in a mirror)

regardless (adv.): whatever may happen; no matter what

regional (adj.): belonging to part of a large area or a part of a country

reliable (adj.): can be counted on to give the same result often; dependable

relieve (v.): lessen pain or trouble

remark (n.): a comment; an idea expressed

remiss (adj.): careless; not doing one's duty

reputation (n.): one's character in the opinion of others

resemble (adj.): look like

reservation (n.): a promise of a table in a restaurant, arranged for future use

retainer (n.): money to hold or reserve someone's services; partial payment in advance

retire (v.): leave activity or an occupation; go to bed

revolution (n.): a complete circular movement around a fixed point (e.g., the revolutions of the moon around the earth)

rib (n.): one of the pairs of bones running around the chest of a person or animal

Riviera (n.): a strip of the Mediterranean coast of southeast France and northwest Italy

roast (n.): a fund-raising event to honor someone by making fun of him/her

rogue (n.): a dishonest or disorderly person

roller skates (n.): shoes with wheels fixed on them, for rolling on a smooth surface

roman numerals (n.): signs used in ancient Rome, and sometimes today, for numbers (I, V, X, etc.)

romantic (adj.): belonging to or suggesting feeling and stories of love and adventure

ruin (v.): to damage irreparably

rural (adj.): of or like the countryside; concerning country or village life

sacred (adj.): religious in nature and use; serious and important, in the way religious things are

scent (n.): a smell, especially as left by an animal, or a pleasant smell from flowers or perfume

scotch (whiskey) (n.): a strong alcoholic drink usually made in Scotland

scrubbing (n.): the act of cleaning by hand; rubbing, often with a stiff brush

second lieutenant (n.): the lowest officer rank in the American army or air force

sensational (adj.): wonderful; very good or exciting; often causing excited interest or attention

sensitive (adj.): delicate; quick to show or feel an effect

shame (v.): painful emotion one feels through guilt or disgrace

signal (v.): be a sign of; give a sound or action that warns, commands, or gives a message

situation comedy (n.): a form of humorous television show with basic characters who appear in different situations each week

sleep-away camp (n.): a place where children live in tents or cabins in the summer and participate in mainly outdoor activities

slop (n.): bad or tasteless food

snack (n.): an amount of food smaller than a meal; something eaten between meals

snarl (v.): make an angry noise

solution (n.): an act or way of finding an answer to a difficulty or problem

sophomore (n.): a student in the second year of high school or college

spa (n.): a fashionable place where people go to lose weight, relax, or be cured of a disease

spotlight (n.): a bright light used in theaters or studios; also used to mean *public attention*

stereo (n.): a record player which gives out sounds from two places by means of two loudspeakers

stereotype (n.): a standardized view of an ethnic or regional group; a set of characteristics thought to apply to all members of the group

stern (adj.): very firm or hard toward others' behavior; showing firmness with disapproval

stork (n.): a large white bird with a long beak, neck, and legs

strategy (n.): skillful planning; a plan for winning success in an activity

stricken (adj.): showing the effect of trouble, anxiety, or illness

stroke (n.): a sudden illness in the brain that damages it, often causing loss of speech or movement

structure (n.): anything formed of many parts, especially a building

stuck (adj.): fixed in place; not moving

suburbs (n.): residential areas just outside or near cities

superstitious (adj.): influenced by a belief that is not based on reason but on magic or old ideas

suspicion (n.): lack of trust or willingness to accept

swallow (v.): action by which one receives something into the body through the mouth and esophagus

swampland (n.): ground that is filled with water, causing buildings to sink

sweat (v.): cool the body by excreting moisture through the openings of the sweat glands of the body

take-out (adj.): referring to goods, especially food, that can be bought and taken away immediately

talk show (n.): a television or radio program in which interesting people are interviewed

teddy bear (n.): a toy bear filled with soft material

tennis outfit (n.): suitable or standard attire for playing the typically outdoor game of tennis

term (n.): a fixed or limited period of time

terminal (n.): a bus station in the center of a town

testimonial (n.): a formal statement of a person's character or ability; something given or done as an expression of respect or thanks

thoroughly (adv.): completely; in every way

threaten (v.): say what will be done to hurt or punish

three-ring circus (n.): a tent with seats for the public around three rings, where animals and skilled or daring people perform

tip (n.): a small amount of money given as a gift for small services

trademark (n.): a special name, sign, behavior, etc., by which a person or activity may be habitually recognized

tranquilizer (n.): a drug used for nervousness and worry

transformer (n.): a toy that can become different things (gun, robot, etc.)

transgression (n.): a wrongdoing; an offense against a moral principle

trial (n.): the act of hearing and judging a person or case in a court of law

trials and tribulations (idiom): tests of one's courage and strength, and causes of grief and worry

trip (v.): catch one's foot and lose one's balance

trustworthy (adj.): dependable; worthy of trust

twist (n.): a sharp unexpected turn

uncivilized (adj.): lacking in education and manners

unemployed (adj.): without a job

unexpected (adj.): unforeseen; cannot be known in advance

unimpressed (adj.): seeing or feeling little about the worth of something

unstable (adj.): easily upset or changed

unveil (v.): uncover

utensil (n.): a small tool for a practical purpose; a household tool

video (n.): a tape of a movie or TV show that can be replayed on a TV

villa (n.): a pleasant country house with a garden, often used only part of the year

villain (n.): a bad person; one who tries to harm others

vodka (n.): a strong, colorless alcoholic drink usually made in northern Europe

wail (v.): make a long cry or sound suggesting grief or pain; complain

weapon (n.): a tool for harming or killing in attack or defense

widow (n.): a woman who has not remarried after her husband died

will (n.): a document that describes how a person's estate is to be handled or split up after his/her death

windbag (n.): a person who talks too much, especially about dull things

wit (n.): the ability to make clever connections in the mind and express them well; cleverness; intelligence

wizard (n.): a very skillful person having almost magical powers

women's liberation movement (n.): a united effort by women to gain equal rights with men, particularly in the workplace

worthy (adj.): deserving of respect and admiration

yelp (v.): make a short sharp cry of pain or excitement